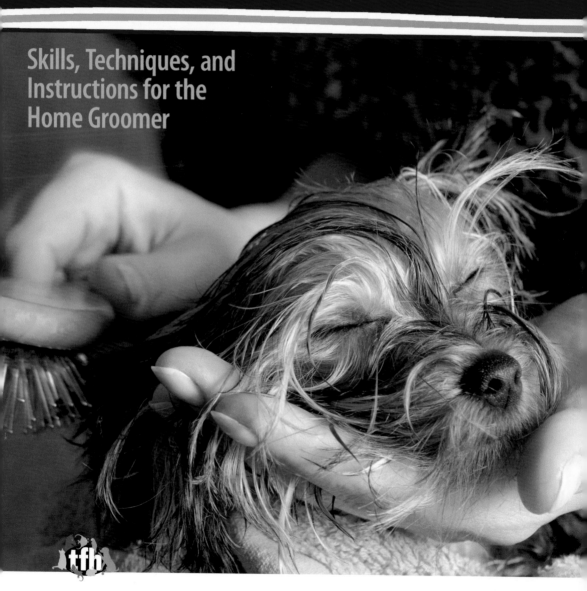

ANIMAL PLANET

COMPLETE GUIDE TO DOG GROOMING

Skills, Techniques, and Instructions for the Home Groomer

tfh

EVE ADAMSON with SANDY ROTH

COMPLETE GUIDE TO DOG GROOMING

Project Team
Editor: Stephanie Fornino
Indexer: Elizabeth Walker
Series Designer: Mary Ann Kahn
Design Layout: Angela Stanford

TFH Publications®
President/CEO: Glen S. Axelrod
Executive Vice President: Mark E. Johnson
Publisher: Christopher T. Reggio
Production Manager: Kathy Bontz

TFH Publications, Inc.®
One TFH Plaza
Third and Union Avenues
Neptune City, NJ 07753

Discovery Communications, LLC. Book Development Team: Marjorie Kaplan, President and General Manager, Animal Planet Media/ Kelly Day, Executive Vice President and General Manager, Discovery Commerce/ Elizabeth Bakacs, Vice President, Licensing and Creative/ JP Stoops, Director, Licensing/ Bridget Stoyko, Associate Art Director, Licensing

 ©2010 Discovery Communications, LLC. Animal Planet and the Animal Planet logo are trademarks of Discovery Communications, LLC, used under license. All rights reserved. *animalplanet.com*

Printed and bound in China
11 12 13 14 15   3 5 7 9 8 6 4 2

Derived from *The Simple Guide to Grooming Your Dog,* originally published in 2003

Library of Congress Cataloging-in-Publication Data
Adamson, Eve.
  Complete guide to dog grooming : skills, techniques, and instructions for the home groomer / Eve Adamson with Sandy Roth.
      p. cm. -- (Animal planet pet care library)
  Rev. ed. of: Simple guide to grooming your dog / Eve Adamson & Sandy Roth, 2003.
  Includes index.
  ISBN 978-0-7938-3714-4 (alk. paper)
  1. Dogs--Grooming. I. Roth, Sandy. II. Adamson, Eve. Simple guide to grooming your dog. III. Title.
  SF427.5.A33 2011
  636.7'083--dc22
                          2011001199

This book has been published with the intent to provide accurate and authoritative information in regard to the subject matter within. While every reasonable precaution has been taken in preparation of this book, the author and publisher expressly disclaim responsibility for any errors, omissions, or adverse effects arising from the use or application of the information contained herein. The techniques and suggestions are used at the reader's discretion and are not to be considered a substitute for veterinary care. If you suspect a medical problem consult your veterinarian.

Note: In the interest of concise writing, "he" is used when referring to puppies and dogs unless the text is specifically referring to females or males. "She" is used when referring to people. However, the information contained herein is equally applicable to both sexes.

The Leader In Responsible Animal Care for Over 50 Years!®
www.tfh.com

CENTRAL
Garden & Pet

CONTENTS

PART ONE

THE IMPORTANCE OF
GOOD GROOMING

GOOD GROOMING = GOOD HEALTH

Humans like to have clear skin, a sweet smell, thick shiny hair, and a really great haircut, and we like our dogs to look and smell great too. But grooming is about more than good looks. Good grooming means great health, for both dogs and humans.

But while you know how to comb your own hair and take a shower, not all pet owners know or understand how to most effectively and efficiently groom their pets. Is your long-coated Shih Tzu a mess of tangles until you shave him down every spring? Is your Schnauzer a disheveled mess of stray wiry hairs? How is your Bearded Collie's skin under all that coat? And what about those wrinkles on your crinkly Pug—are they dry and clean? Are your Beagle's ears free from infection? Have you figured out how to resolve that annoying hot spot on your Labrador Retriever? (And if you think it's annoying, just imagine how your Lab feels!)

Grooming is directly related to health in many ways. A matted coat can hide and aggravate a host of skin conditions, which may in turn signify more serious health problems. A dull or balding coat can reveal medical conditions such as hypothyroidism (symmetric hair loss is a clue), mange (a parasitic condition), or nutritional deficiencies (low protein could mean dull, sparse hair). Dogs with skin folds, floppy ears, furry paw pads, protruding eyes, flat faces, or dental issues all need special kinds of care as well.

Living with a dog is about much more than a daily walk, fresh food, and clean water. To keep your friend at his healthy best, thorough and targeted grooming is in order, and this book is here to help you understand exactly what your pet's individual grooming needs are, as well as how you can best meet them.

ANATOMY AS IT RELATES TO GROOMING

To best groom your dog, it helps to understand a little

To keep your dog at his healthy best, thorough and targeted grooming is necessary.

bit about dog anatomy first. Although a Pug looks a lot different than a Greyhound and a Chihuahua doesn't much resemble a Mastiff, all dogs share the same basic anatomy and many of the same anatomy-related grooming needs. Using the diagram on page 9 for reference, let's consider the dog's anatomy as it relates to grooming.

The Head

A dog's head is an important area for grooming. Some dogs have protruding eyes, some have flat

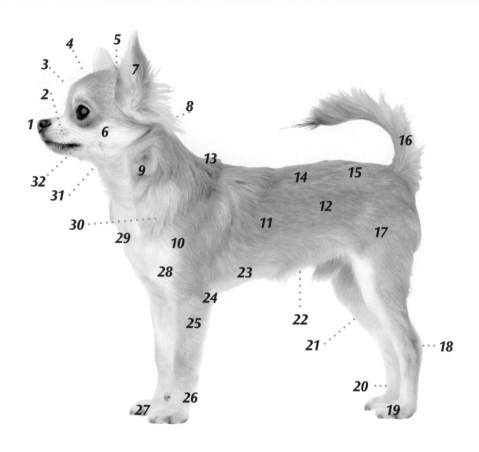

1. Nose	9. Neck	17. Thigh	25. Foreleg
2. Muzzle	10. Shoulder	18. Hock joint	26. Pastern
3. Stop	11. Ribs	19. Rear feet	27. Front feet
4. Skull	12. Loin	20. Metatarsus	28. Upper arm
5. Occiput	13. Withers	21. Stifle	29. Forechest
6. Cheek	14. Back	22. Abdomen	30. Shoulder blade
7. Ear	15. Croup	23. Chest	31. Throat latch
8. Crest of neck	16. Tail or stern	24. Elbow	32. Lip corner

faces, and some have skin wrinkles, and each of these special features requires special grooming. A dog's eyes should be kept clear, eyes and nose checked for discharge, teeth cleaned and checked for excess tartar and gum infection. Dogs with floppy ears are prone to infection because bacteria and moisture can become trapped in the ear, but even prick-eared dogs can get infected or parasite-plagued ears. Dogs whose ears drag along the ground while they are hot on the trail of a scent (like Bloodhounds, Basset Hounds, and Beagles) may also get burs and dirt in and on their ears.

Different dogs have different head shapes. Brachycephalic dogs have flat faces (think Pugs, Pekingese, Bulldogs, and Boston Terriers) and are more likely to have large, sometimes protruding eyes and facial wrinkles. Dogs with longer faces and more deeply set eyes (think Basenjis or Vizslas) may have fewer facial grooming needs but still require vigilance to check for discharge from the eyes and nose as well as for healthy teeth and gums.

To keep your dog's face (no matter what its shape) healthy and well groomed, wipe it clean with a damp cloth and make sure that any folds and wrinkles stay clean and dry, as they can harbor bacteria and can become easily irritated. The flews (the pendulous skin at the corners of the mouth) on the lower lip, especially, need to be cleaned. Whiskers on a dog's muzzle can be trimmed, ear hair can be plucked, and the muzzle can be otherwise neatened, but these are optional, although aesthetically rewarding, grooming chores.

The Body

Your dog's body may be low to the ground or towering, long or short, and covered in just about any kind of coat, from short to long, straight to curly. Although the head and paws may require more targeted grooming time, your dog's body is the realm of the skin and coat and must be tended for a healthy, shiny, vibrant appearance. Brush along the back, the neck, the chest, down each leg, and along the tail, if your dog has a tail. The belly of the male should be kept short for sanitary purposes.

Brushing or combing your dog is an aesthetically pleasing chore and a chance for you to appreciate your breed's unique shape, topline, tail set, and waist. (What, no waist? An overweight dog is prone to many additional health problems, so make good nutrition a partner to good grooming.)

Your dog's coat—his most striking feature—grows in cycles. Each hair follicle has a rapid growth phase, a slower growth phase, a resting phase, and a shedding phase. These phases differ in length according to breed, but most dogs shed or "blow" their coats once or twice a year, and in females, about six to eight weeks after giving birth.

Exposure to daylight can influence the coat growth cycle, so dogs spending a lot of time outdoors are more likely to shed in regular cycles, whereas indoor dogs exposed to about the same light, thermal heat, or air-conditioning all year

Brush Up On a Breed

For more on how to care for your dog's coat, see Part Three for his breed's particular coat type.

round may shed in less obvious cycles and be more likely to shed small amounts all year long.

Some dogs have a double coat, or a soft, woolly undercoat under a harder, shinier outercoat. These double coats offer double protection against the elements for working dogs, but the undercoat can shed in great tufts when the dog sheds.

Some curly-coated breeds don't shed in the same way other dogs shed. Long-coated dogs that shed develop mats more easily because when the long hairs or undercoats shed, they get caught in the longer hair and never drop off, causing tangles. Regular brushing and combing can dramatically reduce the annoyance of shed hair in the house by purposefully removing shed hair before it falls, not to mention minimize the occurrence of mats.

The Feet

Your dog has four paws, and each of those paws must be kept in good condition. Some dogs have tight, compact, rounded cat feet with a shorter third toe. These neat feet are easy to lift and make for greater endurance, as they are efficient for working dogs. Some breeds with cat feet include Doberman Pinschers, Newfoundlands, Finnish Spitz, and Bichons Frises.

Some dogs have hare feet, which are more elongated, with two center toes longer than the side toes. Hare feet make for fast action and

Beauty Tip

Dogs come in a huge range of colors, from white to black, blue to gold, lemon to red, and in many different patterns, from bicolored to tricolored to brindled, spotted, ticked, and roaned. Some grooming supplies are specifically designed to bring out your dog's best color: brightening shampoos for white coats, shampoos designed to bring out the gleam in black coats, and those made just for the lightest straw, the purest blue, or the deepest bronze.

Some water dogs, such as the Flat-Coated Retriever, have webbed feet to help them move through water efficiently.

are characteristic of speedy sighthounds like Greyhounds and Whippets. Other hare-footed breeds include the Samoyed, the Bedlington Terrier, and the Papillon. Many breeds have feet that fall moderately between the cat foot and the hare foot.

Some water dogs, such as the Chesapeake Bay Retriever, the Portuguese Water Dog, and the German Wirehaired Pointer, have webbed feet to help them move efficiently through the water to retrieve game.

Some longhaired breeds grow hair between their foot pads, which should usually be trimmed away to prevent matting and ice caking in the winter, except in the case of some sled dogs, for whom this paw-pad hair serves a protective purpose.

Many dogs are born with dewclaws—fifth toes a few inches (cm) up the leg from the four toes on the floor. This vestigial toe serves no purpose and in many breeds—especially working breeds—the rear dewclaws are removed to prevent them from tearing off by accident. In other breeds, dewclaw removal is purely cosmetic. Many breeders have

the dewclaws removed, except for those breeds that are required to have them, according to their breed standards. All claws, including the dewclaws, should be trimmed.

GROOMING FOR OVERALL HEALTH

We all want our dogs to be healthy, and while genetics, diet, exercise, attention, and mental stimulation all play a part in the big health picture, grooming is one important way you can directly affect your dog's health. A well-groomed dog is likely to maintain a healthier coat, skin, eyes, ears, teeth, and even structure.

Throughout this book we will go into lots of detail about how to groom your dog from nose to tail no matter his size, shape, age, breed, or coat type, but let's look first at how basic grooming can affect his health in specific ways.

Coat Care

The coat is one of the dog's most variable features from one breed to the next. Shave them down and a Standard Poodle, an Afghan Hound, and a German Shorthaired Pointer don't look all that different from each other, but put that Standard Poodle, Afghan Hound, and German Shorthaired Pointer in their full show coats, and you'll see how different similarly sized dogs can look.

One of the most obvious indicators of good health in a dog is his coat. Whether your dog has a long, flowing coat, a mass of frizzy curls, or a sleek, hard coat, its condition is the first thing most people notice, and it may be the first thing to deteriorate when a dog suffers from a health problem.

A poor coat could signify a systemic disease, or it could stem from poor grooming habits, instigating other problems. Caring for your dog's coat does more than keep it in good condition. It keeps you in contact with your dog so that you can catch changes in the coat and skin more quickly. Coats must be washed, although some breeds require more frequent washing than others. They must be brushed as well, and long coats must be periodically detangled. Condition dry coats to keep hair pliable and to keep breakage to a minimum, and when it comes to good health, if you aren't willing to care for a long coat, keep it cut or shaved down. Your pet's comfort and health are more important than sporting a long coat that isn't well groomed.

If you keep your dog's coat well groomed, it should be shiny, fluffy, smooth, clean, and pest-free. You should be able to run a flea comb through it without getting stuck, and it should be pliable and strong enough to resist breakage from regular brushing or combing. This is easy to accomplish by keeping your dog's skin and coat clean. In addition, check periodically for parasites, and run your hands over his entire body at least once a week to check for any lumps, bumps, dry patches, sores, or other skin changes. You may also be able to determine other body issues such as pain in the hips, which could signify hip dysplasia; pain in the

spine, which could signify disc disease; or other joint issues such as arthritis or slipping kneecaps. Just by touching and paying attention to any indications that your dog is in pain, you could catch a serious problem before it becomes much worse.

A well-tended coat free of mats and tangles and kept clean and parasite-free helps reveal skin problems when they begin, rather than hiding them until they are advanced, and will in itself prevent many skin problems from occurring in the first place. But an ungroomed coat can be the catalyst for many different health problems. Let's look at what can happen when you don't properly groom your dog.

Fleas

Fleas can thrive underneath an ungroomed coat, and if you never wash or comb them

If you keep your dog's coat well groomed, it should be shiny, fluffy, smooth, clean, and pest-free.

out, they can breed quickly and infest your entire house. Fleabites can cause dermatitis on your pet, including itchy spots that can become badly infected. Fleas also carry diseases like bubonic plague, and parasites, such as tapeworms, that can infect your dog.

Mats
Those knotty tangles in long coats caused by shed hair that wasn't shed all the way are the result of a lack of adequate grooming or of grooming done improperly. They are more than uncomfortable and unattractive—mats can hide skin problems, from fleas and hot spots to tumors and abscesses.

Poor Hair Quality
Handling your dog's coat too roughly, bathing too often without conditioning, or using tools in the wrong way can result in breakage and brittle hair. Part of good grooming is good nutrition, and an unbalanced diet can also result in dry, brittle hair that breaks easily and looks dull and lifeless. Poor coat quality can also be a symptom of an underlying health issue.

Ticks
These bloodsucking arachnids look like harmless little beetles until they attach to your dog and swell with blood. Ticks contain harmful bacteria that can even infect humans if they burst during removal. They can also spread diseases to both dogs and humans, such as Lyme disease and Rocky Mountain spotted fever. If a tick is removed improperly, it can leave its head inside your dog, and the wound can become infected.

Skin Care
Underneath all that coat is your dog's largest organ: his skin. Coat care and skin care go hand in hand, and when one is healthy, the other is likely to be healthy too. However, some breeds are more likely than others to suffer from skin problems, including allergies and reactions to irritants like fleabites,

shampoos, and other environmental agents.

Some dogs have very dry skin or allergy-prone skin, and some breeds (such as certain scenthounds) secrete oils that give them a strong odor if they aren't bathed frequently. Some dogs are prone to benign cysts, especially when they age; cysts and sores can also indicate certain serious medical conditions.

Dogs with white coats are prone to sunburn and should be sprayed with sunscreen made just for dogs. Dogs with black coats can easily become overheated, and moles and other skin abnormalities, including fleas and ticks, may be less obvious on a dark-coated dog.

Any dog can develop skin cancer, especially those who spend a lot of time outside, so part of grooming should include a once-over to check the skin for changes. According to one estimate, 450 out of every 100,000 dogs is diagnosed with skin cancer, and light-coated dogs are more susceptible than those with dark coats, in the same way that light-skinned people are more susceptible to skin cancer than dark-skinned people. Skin cancer is the most common type of cancer in dogs, so keep an eye out and talk to your vet about any suspicious moles, lesions, lumps, or other skin changes on your dog.

Ears, Eyes, Nose, and Teeth

You love your dog's beautiful face, and good grooming will keep it beautiful and healthy. But there are a few things you should be aware of to keep that face looking its best. (More on how to care for the eyes, ears, nose, and teeth is discussed in Part Two.)

> **Dogs with white coats are prone to sunburn and should be sprayed with doggy sunscreen.**

Ears

Dogs with long, floppy ears need special ear care to prevent infection, but all dogs can use an occasional ear cleaning. For dogs whose ears tend to grow hair, ear plucking will neaten the appearance of the head and can also prevent dirt and foreign matter from becoming trapped in the ear.

Eyes

Eyes can tear, and many white dogs such as Maltese and white Poodles may develop tearstains. Other breeds with more protruding eyes, such as the Shih Tzu, tend to have dry eyes and may need a daily dose of moisturizing eyedrops to keep their eyes comfortable and healthy. Dogs with large, protruding eyes also require caution during grooming, as their eyes are relatively unprotected and could be injured with a misjudged manipulation of a grooming tool.

Heel!

All dogs walk on their toes in the manner of a horse instead of on the "soles" of their "feet" like humans do. This means that the dog's true "heel" is up in the air, not on the ground. The dog's paw is equivalent to the toes and ball of the human foot.

Nose

Check your dog's nose for discharge, which could indicate a respiratory problem or allergic reaction.

Teeth

Keep your dog's teeth clean; dental bacteria can travel to the heart, where it can be deadly. Daily teeth brushing can help maintain a healthy mouth, as can chew toys and dental treats.

Claws and Paws

When claws get too long, they can compromise movement by bending the foot back too much and splaying out the toes. Too much walking on too-long toenails can eventually cripple a dog. Sharp claws can also do damage to human skin.

Paw pads can become cracked and dry in dry weather or after walks on snow and ice. De-icing salt can also irritate or even damage a dog's paw pads, so keep paws neat, clean, and dry. Clip nails parallel to the ground, avoiding the vein, known as the quick, that extends partway down each nail.

Many white dogs, such as the Maltese, may develop tearstains.

Keep your dog's teeth clean—daily teeth brushing can help maintain a healthy mouth.

A more detailed description of how to clip your dog's nails is discussed in Part Two.

Rears

One part of your dog's body that you may not be so inclined to examine thoroughly is the rear end. Dogs with long hair can develop mats in the rear area, trapping fecal matter, and this area should be kept clipped and clean. All dogs also have anal glands that should empty on their own during defecation, but if your dog becomes irritated in this area or starts scooting around on the floor, these sacs may need to be emptied by hand. (This is a common problem in many dogs.) It's not a pretty job, but it isn't difficult either. Ask your vet to demonstrate how to squeeze the fluid from these sacs. (If you take your dog to be professionally groomed, don't expect your groomer to do this job,

and if she does, well…give her a nice tip!)

More on how to care for your dog's back end can be found in Part Two.

YOUR ALLY, THE VET

Finally, no discussion of grooming for health would be complete without a note about your friendly neighborhood veterinarian. Regular vet care is essential to any pet's good health, but a vet can do more than vaccinations and a once-over. If you have questions about hygiene, concerns about odor or lumps or hair loss or tooth decay, or any other questions regarding your pet's skin, coat, nails, ears, or any other aspect of his anatomy, even if it seems purely cosmetic, don't hesitate to ask your vet. She may also be able to recommend a competent and experienced groomer to help you keep your pet looking his bright and shiny best.

2

DIFFERENT COATS FOR DIFFERENT FOLKS

What dog coat strikes your fancy? Do you adore the long flowing silk of a Yorkshire Terrier, or do you swoon over the powderpuff head of a Bichon Frise? Maybe you admire the elegance of the Doberman's shiny, hard coat or are charmed by the whiskery, wiry look of a Schnauzer.

f you are reading this book, you probably already have a dog. Did you consider coat type when researching breeds? Coat type is an important consideration in choosing your pet because different coat types require drastically different grooming techniques—techniques you may or may not be willing to perform (or pay someone else to perform). You can brush down your Whippet with barely any effort, but to groom a Poodle on your own is a massive undertaking that most pet owners prefer to delegate to a professional groomer (although learning to do it yourself can also be a lot of fun!).

In this chapter we will look at the five basic coat types and talk about the nature of each coat and what that means for the home groomer: you! Later we will devote a chapter to the nuts and bolts of grooming each coat type, but here we'll get ready by looking at the coats themselves, the breeds that sport them, and how much care they involve.

1.) SMOOTH COAT

Smooth coats are shiny, sleek, and almost give the appearance of gleaming skin. They fit so closely that they don't interfere in any way with the sleek silhouettes of the breeds that sport them. Some smooth-coated breeds have single coats and some have double coats, but undercoats shouldn't show through the hard outercoat. Smooth coats are easy to groom: Just brush, polish, and go.

Smooth-Coated Breeds

- American Foxhound
- American Staffordshire Terrier
- Anatolian Shepherd
- Basenji
- Basset Hound
- Beagle
- Black and Tan Coonhound
- Bloodhound
- Boston Terrier
- Boxer
- Bulldog
- Bullmastiff
- Bull Terrier
- Chihuahua (smooth)
- Chinese Shar-Pei
- Chinese Crested
- Dalmatian
- Dachshund (Smooth)
- Doberman Pinscher
- English Foxhound
- Fox Terrier (smooth)
- French Bulldog
- German Shorthaired Pointer
- Great Dane
- Greater Swiss Mountain Dog
- Greyhound
- Harrier
- Ibizan Hound
- Italian Greyhound
- Jack and Parson Russell Terriers (smooth)
- Labrador Retriever
- Manchester Terrier (Toy and Standard)
- Mastiff
- Miniature Pinscher
- Pointer
- Pharaoh Hound
- Pug
- Rhodesian Ridgeback
- Rottweiler
- Staffordshire Bull Terrier
- Toy Fox Terrier
- Vizsla
- Weimaraner
- Whippet

Every group of purebred dogs, from sporting dogs to working dogs, terriers to toys, includes breeds with smooth coats. Although they don't offer much protection from the elements compared to some other coat types, smooth coats also don't interfere with work, don't attract burs, don't catch in underbrush, and don't tangle or mat.

Dogs with smooth coats are also easier to care for in many ways. Wounds and parasites are easily visible and easily removable on a smooth coat, and smooth hard coats shed dried mud and debris with little more than a good shake. Unless they get into something really nasty, smooth-coated breeds don't normally require bathing more than three or four times each year (with the exception of working, hunting, or athletic dogs who spend a lot of time outdoors getting dirty). Too much bathing can strip the oils from the skin of smooth-coated dogs, leaving skin more vulnerable and the coat dull. However, because smooth coats don't offer much skin protection, some of these breeds may develop irritated skin, and some are prone to skin allergies.

To keep smooth coats glossy, brush with a regular, natural bristle brush or a hound glove. A rubber curry brush can also help loosen excess coat during shedding. Unlike heavier double-coated breeds and breeds with longer coats, smooth coats don't require blow-drying, although a professional groomer may dry the smooth coats with a cage dryer to speed up drying. Smooth coats generally dry quickly, however.

Smooth-coated breeds are perfect for people who don't want to spend much time grooming

and who appreciate the clearly defined shape of the dog unencumbered by hair. Except for the occasional whisker trim, smooth-coated breeds are shown in dog shows "naturally," meaning their coats aren't groomed or shaped in any way.

> Dogs with smooth coats are easier to care for in many ways than dogs with longer coats.

2.) MEDIUM COAT

Medium-coated breeds are also easy to groom. Their coats are generally longer than 1 inch (2.5 cm) but are by no means long. Medium-coated dogs don't generally develop mats, although thick

Medium-Coated Breeds

- Akita
- Alaskan Malamute
- American Eskimo Dog
- Australian Cattle Dog
- Australian Shepherd
- Belgian Malinois
- Belgian Sheepdog
- Belgian Tervuren
- Bernese Mountain Dog
- Borzoi
- Border Collie
- Brittany
- Canaan Dog
- Cardigan Welsh Corgi
- Cavalier King Charles Spaniel
- Chesapeake Bay Retriever
- Clumber Spaniel
- Collie (smooth)
- English Springer Spaniel
- Field Spaniel
- Finnish Spitz
- Flat-Coated Retriever
- German Shepherd Dog
- Golden Retriever
- Great Pyrenees
- Kuvasz
- Norwegian Elkhound
- Pembroke Welsh Corgi
- Saint Bernard
- Saluki
- Schipperke
- Shiba Inu
- Siberian Husky
- Spinone Italiano
- Sussex Spaniel
- Tibetan Spaniel
- Welsh Springer Spaniel

double coats of this length could develop mats if they aren't brushed out once a week. In medium-coated dogs, the coat does stand out as part of the silhouette, but these breeds are also generally shown in natural form in the show ring rather than requiring lots of trimming and other coat alterations.

Medium coats vary, from the silky feathers of a Golden Retriever to the plush fur of a Dandie Dinmont Terrier, from the well-insulated Alaskan Malamute to the weather-resistant German Shepherd Dog. While medium-coated breeds may differ greatly from one breed to another, they all have one thing in common: a thick, weather-resistant coat evolved for survival in the elements (ice and snow, underbrush, or lake water). Many working and herding dogs have medium coats because they are easy to care for and don't interfere with the work at hand (or paw) but are

thick enough to offer protection against cold and rain. Double-coated medium-length coats are extra warm and water repellent.

Brush medium coats thoroughly once a week, and when parasites are a problem, apply a flea comb. Otherwise, these coats virtually take care of themselves—and the dogs who wear them. Medium-coated breeds are perfect for people who don't want to do much grooming and those who like larger dogs—many of the larger working, sporting, and herding breeds have medium coats. Medium-coated dogs are soft to the touch and easy to pet, perfectly embodying many people's idea of the perfect dog.

3.) LONG COAT

The long coat is the grooming aficionado's dream coat. Witness any devoted groomer brushing out a Yorkshire Terrier, an Afghan Hound, or a Pekingese, and you'll know what we mean—

and if you have a long-coated dog, you already know what we mean! Grooming a long coat is time consuming but rewarding because the end result—a glamorous, flowing mane—is nothing short of breathtaking.

Some long coats are parted down the back and some aren't. Some are long and frizzy like a Chow Chow or a Pomeranian or fluffy all over like a Collie or a Saint Bernard. Some have shorter coats along the back but long feathers along the underside, ears, and tail, like an English Setter. Long coats are a lot like human hair, and brushing and combing them can be quite similar to brushing and combing your own hair.

Why do dogs have long coats? Theories abound, but some believe that herding dogs tended to have long white coats to better blend in with flocks of sheep, and sheep-like coats offered protection from the elements. Some toy dogs probably evolved to have long, luxurious coats for the sake of the

Long-Coated Breeds

- Afghan Hound
- Bearded Collie
- Briard
- Chihuahua (longhaired)
- Chinese Crested (powderpuff)
- Chow Chow
- Cocker Spaniel
- Collie (rough)
- Dachshund (Longhaired)
- English Cocker Spaniel
- English Setter
- English Toy Spaniel
- Gordon Setter
- Havanese
- Irish Setter
- Japanese Chin
- Keeshond
- Lhasa Apso
- Löwchen
- Maltese
- Newfoundland
- Old English Sheepdog
- Papillon
- Pekingese
- Polish Lowland Sheepdog
- Pomeranian
- Saint Bernard (longhaired)
- Samoyed
- Shetland Sheepdog
- Shih Tzu
- Silky Terrier
- Skye Terrier
- Tibetan Terrier
- Yorkshire Terrier

amusement of the royalty that kept and bred them to make them look regal and pampered. Over the centuries, as different breeds evolved, long-coated breeds were probably selected for their beauty,

as humans have long appreciated the aesthetic pleasures of a long-coated dog, whether on the hunt or riding around in the sleeve of a kimono.

Long coats do need fastidious attention every day or at least every couple of days. Brush them, then comb with a flea comb to make sure that all tangles are removed. Tangles left untended can trap shed hairs and quickly turn to mats, and a long-coated dog with a matted coat is a sorry sight. Long coats also need bathing much more frequently than smooth coats, which require the skin's natural oils to maintain shiny health. Long-coated dogs are at greater risk for tangles, and a monthly bath, conditioning, and blowout will keep this challenging coat type in great shape.

Some long-coated dogs have long *long* coats, and some have coats that need lots of care but aren't quite as taxing to groom. Your Bearded Collie or Afghan Hound will take a lot more combing than your longhaired Chihuahua or Papillon.

Long-coated dogs are perfect for people who love to spend lots of time doting on their pet via

Long coats require fastidious attention at least every couple of days.

Wirehaired/Broken-Coated Breeds

- Affenpinscher
- Airedale Terrier
- Australian Terrier
- Border Terrier
- Bouvier des Flandres
- Brussels Griffon
- Cairn Terrier
- Dachshund (Wirehaired)
- Dandie Dinmont Terrier
- Fox Terrier (wire)
- German Wirehaired Pointer
- Irish Terrier
- Irish Wolfhound
- Jack and Parson Russell Terriers (wirehaired)
- Lakeland Terrier
- Norfolk Terrier
- Norwich Terrier
- Otterhound
- Petit Basset Griffon Vendeen
- Schnauzer: Giant, Standard, and Miniature
- Scottish Deerhound
- Scottish Terrier
- Sealyham Terrier
- Soft Coated Wheaten Terrier
- Welsh Terrier
- West Highland White Terrier
- Wirehaired Pointing Griffon

long grooming sessions. These sessions can be great ways for people and pets to bond. However, if you aren't up for the big grooming commitment but your heart is set on that Shih Tzu, Lhasa Apso, or Maltese, consider keeping your pet in a puppy cut or other short pet trim. For a show dog, only the most glorious of long coats will do, but for a beloved pet, coat length won't affect how much your dog loves you.

4.) WIREHAIRED/BROKEN COAT

The wirehaired or broken coat has a texture all its

Brush Up On a Breed

How a curly coat will be groomed is largely a matter of fashion and practicality for an individual breed. The Poodle's characteristic balls of fur around his joints originally served the function of protecting joints from cold water because the breed was once a water retriever. The Poodle wasn't left in full coat because its sheer weight would have made swimming difficult—even impossible.

own: hard, coarse, and wiry. Wirehaired breeds are often groomed to sport jaunty beards, and their coats have a characteristic tousled look that some of us find irresistible.

Many terrier breeds have a wire coat, and so do a few sporting dogs and hounds. Wire coats are incredibly weather resistant. They defy burs to stick in them and offer good protection for those dogs whose function often involved plummeting through harsh bracken, into burows, or through fields in harsh climates after vermin, whether rats, badgers, or deer.

The unique feature of a wire coat is that to keep it properly harsh and crisp, it should never be shaved down. Instead, it should be stripped or plucked, a process in which dead hairs are pulled by hand or with a stripping knife from the coat. Shaving down a wire coat can result in a softer, less characteristic texture, so wirehaired show dogs are almost always

Curly-Coated Breeds

- American Water Spaniel
- Bedlington Terrier
- Bichon Frise
- Curly-Coated Retriever
- Irish Water Spaniel
- Kerry Blue Terrier
- Komondor
- Poodle: Standard, Miniature, and Toy
- Portuguese Water Dog
- Puli

lovingly hand-stripped by their owners, handlers, and/or groomers.

People who love the look of a wirehaired dog may enjoy the satisfying task of hand-stripping, either a lot at a time several times a year or a little bit at a time all year long. However, if you love your wirehaired friend but don't want to engage in the time-consuming effort of hand-stripping him, periodic clipping and the resultant softer coat may be a perfectly acceptable option.

5.) CURLY/WAVY COAT

So few breeds with curly coats, but *so much grooming!* Although curls characterize just a handful of breeds, they present a unique grooming challenge. Most pet owners take their curly-coated pets to a professional groomer because the grooming of a curly coat is difficult and takes practice. Luckily, the curly coat grows back in quickly, making it the perfect canvas for the novice groomer. You can practice…and practice…and practice until you achieve perfection.

Groomers spend much of their time learning how to groom a single breed: Poodles! Whole books have been written about Poodle grooming. (You won't find a whole book devoted to grooming the Labrador Retriever!) Grooming a curly coat takes skill with a clipper and scissors to achieve the clip of choice.

Some curly-coated breeds sport dreadlocks. The large white Komondor and the diminutive Puli are two distinctively corded breeds with curly coats that fall naturally into cords—and who would look a lot like Poodles if they were groomed that way. Similarly, a Poodle could wear a corded coat if his curls were allowed to form into cords, and in fact, the corded Poodle was in fashion in the 19th century.

Curly coats are common in water dogs because they are so effective at repelling water

and insulating their wearers. Along with the Poodle, other water dogs with curly coats include the Curly-Coated Retriever, the Portuguese Water Dog, and the American and Irish Water Spaniels.

Curly-coated breeds are perfect for people who either don't mind paying a groomer once a month to groom their pets or for those who want to learn all about the art of grooming curly coats. If you love the look, you may appreciate your pet's curly coat even more if you learn to take care of it yourself.

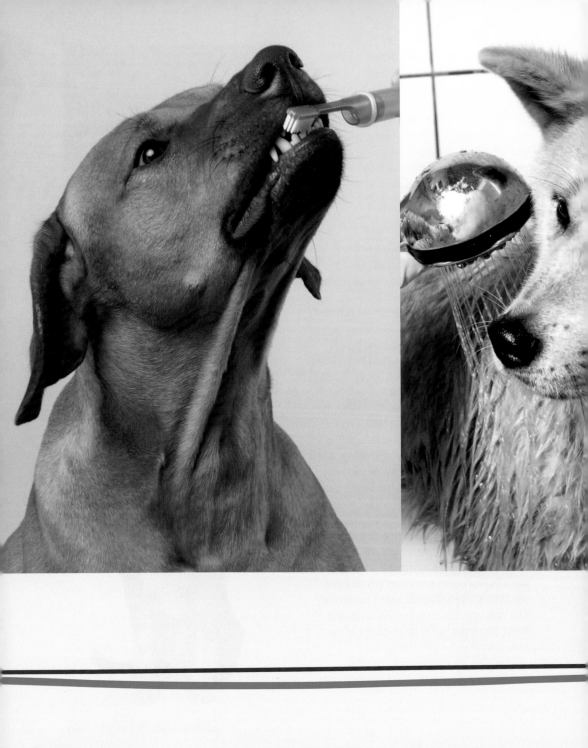

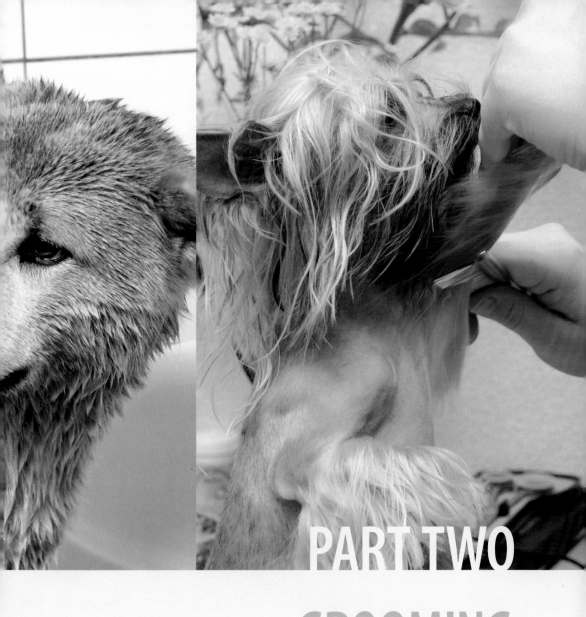

PART TWO

GROOMING

BASICS

3

GETTING STARTED

Ready for the nuts and bolts of grooming setup? It's time to get organized, set up a grooming station, plan your schedule, buy your supplies, and map out your grooming routine. Although some dogs will be fine if you brush them whenever you think about it and trim their nails when you notice they are getting a little too long, most will benefit from a regular grooming routine in a comfortable environment, designed to suit their individual needs with the right equipment and supplies.

very home groomer should have a comfortable, well-lit location for pet grooming, easily accessible supplies, and a good system for keeping records. In this chapter, you'll learn the basics of a home grooming setup. Good grooming begins with good planning, and this chapter will help get you started.

DESIGN YOUR PLAN

Dogs thrive on routine, and even the most easygoing may be thrown off by sporadic grooming. ("Uh-oh, is she or isn't she going for those nail trimmers! Run away! Run away!") However, dogs who learn that grooming is a weekly or even a daily part of the schedule will accept it more readily, and many will look forward to it as a special time to spend with their owners. ("Hey, that brushing feels pretty good! Don't stop!")

Making grooming a habit is your responsibility and your challenge. Commit to grooming the same way you commit to brushing your teeth or paying your bills, and it will soon become a regular part of your routine. Whether your regular grooming sessions (brushing, combing, eyes, ears, and teeth) happen daily or weekly, schedule your sessions and allow a monthly longer session (for example, the first or last Sunday of each month) for more detailed attention to your pet's grooming needs. You are responsible for his health and well-being.

Most dogs benefit from a regular grooming routine in a comfortable environment.

Grooming consists of two basic levels, which we will call Level I and Level II for the purpose of this book. Each level is a necessary part of your dog's grooming routine: Level I is for basic maintenance, and Level II includes a bath and a more thorough check, as well as clipping and styling of the coat.

Some people choose to do Level I grooming themselves but leave Level II grooming to the professional groomer. Others enjoy learning how to do Level II grooming themselves. Let's look at what each level involves so that you can best incorporate all necessary grooming steps into your routine.

Level I Grooming

Level I is the kind of grooming you do every few days to keep your dog in good shape: brushing, combing, checking the body for changes, cleaning the teeth (which you should ideally do daily), and perhaps clipping off toenail tips. Although some people do this kind of maintenance once a week or even less often, a daily grooming session is a pleasant and effective way to bond with your pet. No, your dog's coat might not need to be brushed every day, but that doesn't mean that you *can't* brush it every day, and every pet will benefit from a little pampering on a daily basis. (Wouldn't we all?)

Level I grooming generally consists of the following steps (although you can certainly alter these to fit your individual pet and situation):

- coat massage to stimulate skin and check for lumps, bumps, sores, rashes, and other skin changes
- all-over brushing
- quick run-through with a comb to check for fleas and any missed tangles
- ear check
- eye check
- wipe-down of face and eyes with a moist, clean

Table It

A grooming table is a valuable tool for a professional groomer, but home groomers may also find grooming much easier if they use one. Standard grooming tables are approximately 2 feet by 3 feet (.5 m by 1 m), but smaller tables are also available for toy breeds. Grooming tables have nonskid surfaces, and many come with grooming posts or arms so that dogs can be secured to a leash, and for larger dogs, a belly band. These posts keep dogs feeling secure and protect against escape before they are used to staying put for grooming. Grooming tables generally sell for less than a few hundred dollars for basic models.

cloth and application of eye drops if necessary (for breeds with tendency toward dry eyes)
- brush or wipe-down of teeth
- check and handling of each paw, clipping off toenail tips if necessary
- a notation in your grooming journal about what you did and how your pet looks and acts today (see the last section in this chapter for more on your grooming journal)
- a treat for being *such* a good dog

Again, consider a Level I grooming session every day at the same time each day, perhaps right after your own morning grooming session or as a way to bond with your pet and wind down in the evening after a long day. Your relationship with him will surely benefit, and you will be sure to catch any physical and/or behavioral changes in your dog as soon as they occur. If you don't choose to groom at this level every day, do so at least once a week for smooth, medium, wire, and curly-coated breeds and three or four times a week for long-coated breeds. Dogs are usually more cooperative in the evening or after a nice long walk.

Level II Grooming

Level II grooming is the kind of grooming pets need every few months. For long-coated, curly-coated, wirehaired, and medium-coated breeds in full show coats, Level II grooming is best done every four to six weeks. For smooth-coated dogs, Level II grooming every two months is fine, with a bath even less often. A Level II grooming session usually consists of the following steps (again, vary these according to the needs of your pet and your situation):

- more thorough check of skin, eyes, ears, teeth, rear, paws, and paw pads
- parasite check and pesticide application when necessary
- thorough brush-out with tangle and mat removal
- thorough comb-out to ensure that all tangles and mats are out of the coat
- bath and coat-conditioning treatment
- clipping and styling of coat as appropriate for breed
- nail clipping
- application of eye drops and ear powder
- tooth scaling and anal gland expressing, both as necessary

If you choose to take your dog to a professional groomer for this level of grooming because you don't want to do the bathing, clipping, and styling yourself, that's fine. Professional groomers are widely available, and some have even hit the road in mobile grooming vans that will come to your house and groom your dog right in your own driveway. Or

you may find that you enjoy grooming your dog so much that you would like to become a professional groomer yourself. To learn more about this fun and flexible career, check out Part Five.

A daily grooming session is a pleasant and effective way to bond with your pet.

SET UP YOUR GROOMING STATION

The grooming station is the heart of your grooming routine. If you don't have a good place to groom your dog, you probably won't bother until grooming has become an emergency. A workable grooming station can be as simple or as elaborate as you want to make it. You can transform a spare room into a grooming center or groom on the deck or porch where hair can fly without necessitating cleanup. You can invest in a grooming table or groom on the counter (for a small dog) or on the floor (for a large dog) of your bathroom. You can also use a nonskid bathmat on top of a washer or dryer. It doesn't matter where you groom as long as you have a station that makes it easy.

Choose a Location

Finding a good place to groom your dog can make all the difference in actually establishing the habit. A location for grooming that is convenient and pleasant will be conducive to the regular practice of

Clipping and styling your dog's coat should be done every four to six weeks.

Beauty Tip

Keep your brushes and combs in good condition. When bristles begin to bend, pins fall out, or comb teeth break off, replace your tools or you could risk damaging your dog's coat and even his skin.

grooming your dog. Where will you be most likely to groom him regularly? There are some things to consider.

First, how much cleanup will your dog require? The mess your grooming sessions will make can determine where to groom. For example,

longhaired dogs whose coat stays in the comb are easy to groom indoors, but brushing your short-coated shedder may release tiny hairs into the air, so you may prefer an outdoor location. A harsh climate makes outdoor grooming inconvenient during much of the year; a temperate climate is more conducive to outdoor grooming.

Also, that spare room or basement might be a great grooming studio unless it is stuffy, uncomfortable, or dim or you have to make an extra trip up or down stairs that you probably won't be willing to make.

The ideal grooming location has plenty of lighting, is big enough to move around in, and is easy to clean. Whether you use a corner of your bathroom or the front step, choose a location and use it every time. Your dog will soon associate that location with grooming and will be comfortable and secure in knowing exactly what is going to happen in that spot. Sticking with one location will make grooming easier on everyone.

Organize Your Grooming Station

Once you've secured a location, it's time to organize your grooming station. If grooming is a well-organized affair, it will be a pleasure, but if you have to spend 20 minutes looking for that brush—and where did you put those nail clippers?—you may be less inclined to bother.

If you have a small dog, you will need a raised surface on which to groom. Stooping down for half an hour to comb out your Shih Tzu is uncomfortable and hardly ergonomic. A grooming table can be a wonderful piece of equipment if you have space for it and choose to invest in one. Grooming tables put dogs at a comfortable grooming height and are covered in a nonskid surface so that your dog can stand easily and safely. Or put your toy dog on a bathroom counter on a towel or bathmat. A larger dog can stand on the floor as you sit on a stool or chair. Try different setups until you find one that works for you and your dog.

Next, organize your tools: brush, comb, clippers, and whatever else you will need for your dog. (See the next section for notes on tool selection.) Put them in a basket or set of baskets, or organize them in a container made to organize office or other tools. Keep in mind that you should be able to see what you need so that you can reach that item easily.

All breeds and coat types can benefit from grooming with a natural bristle brush.

Finally, store the tools in a convenient location: a cabinet, a counter, or anywhere with easy access to your grooming area. If seeing the grooming tools will help you remember to groom, place them in plain sight. If clutter bugs you, stash them away, but be sure that they are easy to grab when you need them.

Assemble Your Tools

You will need certain tools to groom your pet, and what kind of tools you need depends on what kind of pet you have. All dogs have certain supplies and equipment in common, but long coats require different grooming tools than smooth coats, wire coats, curly coats, etc.

Later in this book, as we talk about grooming different coat types, we'll talk more about the individual tools you will need for certain coat types. But to get you started, the following is a general list of the tools you will need for grooming.

For All Breeds and Coat Types

- combination medium/fine-toothed comb
- nail file for smoothing rough nails
- nail trimmers of appropriate size made for use on dogs
- natural bristle brush
- small curved and/or blunt-tipped scissors for whisker and foot trimming

Optional Tools

These tools are for grooming beyond what is necessary for a pet. If you want to groom a show dog or just want to groom precisely according to the grooming protocol for a show dog, you might also want to invest in the following.

- ear forceps for removing ear hair
- grooming table
- nail grinder/dremel tool for filing nails

- nonskid rubber mat for bathing and grooming
- showerhead hose attachment for easier bathing
- terrier mitt (for terriers)
- thinning shears

For Smooth Coats

Grooming the smooth-coated dog centers around good health, a shiny coat, and the accentuation of the breed's unique silhouette. Invest in the following:

- blow-dryer with cool setting (optional but good for small, easily chilled breeds like Chihuahuas and Italian Greyhounds)
- chamois, flannel, silk, or velvet squares for polishing
- clippers with #10 blade for occasional neatening, depending on breed
- hound glove
- rubber curry brush

For Medium Coats

Grooming the medium-coated dog is easy, as most medium-coated breeds are supposed to appear naturally without alteration. Brush, trim nails, clean ears, trim hair on feet and ears, and you're done! Invest in the following:

- blow-dryer with cool setting
- coat rake
- hound glove
- pin brush
- rubber curry brush
- shedding comb

For Long Coats

Grooming the long-coated dog is largely centered around coat care and detangling. Invest in the following:

- blow-dryer with cool setting
- clippers with a variety of blade sizes as relevant for breed (some long-coated breeds require clipping, while others don't)
- mat comb
- mat splitter
- pin brush
- rubber bands, bows, ribbons, barrettes, etc., for those long-coated dogs with topknots
- scissors, for shaping and trimming
- shedding comb
- slicker brush

- wide-toothed comb for thickly coated breeds (such as Collies and Samoyeds)

For Wire Coats

Grooming the wire coat requires brushing and plucking or stripping to remove dead hairs, keeping the coat healthy and bright. Invest in the following:

- blow-dryer with cool setting
- combination medium/fine-toothed comb
- electric clippers with a variety of blade sizes as relevant for breed, for shaping and keeping anal area clean

Grooming the long-coated dog is largely centered around coat care and detangling.

- hound glove
- natural bristle brush
- scissors, for shaping and trimming
- shedding comb
- slicker brush
- stripping knife

For Curly Coats

For crisp, marcelled curls (continuous waves), never brush that curly coat after a bath! Wash, condition, shape, and dry. Some curly coats with a more powder-puff appearance are brushed and combed, so technique depends on your breed's particular look and clip.

- coat rake
- combination medium/fine-toothed metal comb
- electric clippers with a variety of blade sizes as relevant for breed, for shaping and keeping anal area clean
- natural bristle brush
- pin brush
- scissors, for shaping and trimming

- shedding comb
- slicker brush

Decide on Products

Although you can customize your product selection to your breed and to those products you want to use, this is a general list of the kinds of products you will want to consider for stocking your grooming station. The products listed as necessary form the basis of good grooming. Optional products are for those home groomers who want to go the extra mile.

> It's easy to groom smooth- and medium-coated breeds because most are supposed to appear naturally without alteration.

Necessary Products

- coat conditioner for your dog's coat type
- cotton balls
- eye drops for moistening and cleaning eyes
- petroleum jelly to protect eyes and ears
- medicated ear powder or other ear cleaning

liquid, such as rubbing alcohol or a product designed for this purpose

- nail coagulant or styptic pencil
- shampoo for your dog's coat type

Optional Products

- cologne or other scented coat spray
- lanolin or oil-based coat spray, for sheen
- mineral oil for polishing nails
- talcum powder, for keeping skin wrinkles dry

KEEP A GROOMING JOURNAL

The last aspect of grooming preparation is to establish a grooming journal. The grooming journal will become an invaluable record of your pet's health. In it, you can record what you do at each grooming session, as well as keep a record of each vet visit, changes in your dog's habits and behavior, what you feed your dog, how much your dog eats and drinks each day, and anything you notice during grooming sessions: sensitive areas, lumps, bumps, rashes, sores, coat changes, dental changes, etc.

Depending on how much time you spend on your grooming journal, you can also devote space to recording funny stories about the things your pet does each day. Include photos of your pet, from puppyhood through the senior years. Always bring your grooming journal to the vet with you so that you can write down all tests, shots, advice, and suggested vaccination schedules you may forget. Let your grooming journal be a record of your pet's life, and you may be surprised how often you refer to it.

Choose a sturdy book with plenty of pages. Organize your journal in whatever way works for you. Maybe you prefer a binder with sections for grooming dates/notes, veterinary information, diet, and behavior notes. Maybe a bound book with blank pages is more your style, or perhaps you will keep a journal on your computer.

Now you're ready to start grooming. The next section of this book will take you through the basics of actually grooming your pet, from brush-out and bath to the finishing touches.

Brush That Puppy!

Although some dogs balk at having their nails trimmed, teeth brushed, or coat combed, dogs trained from puppyhood that grooming is part of the regular routine are a dream to groom. They have learned that good grooming is a part of life, and they would never think to argue about it! Diligent pet owners will soon discover that a dog accustomed to regular grooming is much better behaved for veterinary examinations too.

Begin with two- to three-minute grooming sessions and gradually build up the time in small increments. For a puppy, give a treat while each foot is being handled. Always give the treats while he is in the grooming location so that he associates something good with each session. The treats can be something special, or for a puppy at risk for too-quick weight gain, they can be part of his food portion for the day.

4

THE PRE-BATH BRUSH-OUT

In the next few chapters, we will take you through the initial steps involved in the Level II grooming session: the thorough brush-out, the bath, and the finishing touches on your dog. (Part Three of this book will look at clipping, trimming, and styling, as well as more detailed advice on caring for individual coat types.)

The heart and soul of your Level II grooming session is the brush-out. Brushing is indeed at the very core of grooming. No matter what coat type your dog has, brushing and combing every few days will keep shedding to a minimum, stimulate the skin, and keep the coat shiny and healthy. A neglected coat is a coat that is never brushed, but a frequently brushed coat is a joy to behold, whether worn by a Labrador Retriever or a Lhasa Apso.

But before a bath, grooming is particularly important. Water will tighten

A pre-bath brush-out removes shed coat, loosens dead skin, distributes natural oils, and prepares the coat so that bathing will be most effective.

and worsen mats and tangles, so this pre-bath brush-out is essential for removing mats. Even in dogs with shorter coats, a pre-bath brush-out will remove shed coat, loosen dead skin, distribute natural oils, and prepare the coat so that bathing will be most effective. Use a spray bottle with water or coat conditioner to keep the coat slightly damp while brushing and combing. This will also help eliminate static electricity.

READY YOUR TOOLS

You will use most of your grooming tools during the brush-out, according to your dog's coat type: your comb, hound glove, mat comb/mat splitter/ coat rake, natural bristle brush, pin brush, slicker brush, rubber curry brush, and/or any other brush

serve the same purpose: to remove all tangles after brushing. Combs should feel comfortable in your hand, and metal combs with rounded teeth are sturdy and gentle on skin. In dogs prone to static electricity, try a wooden comb.

- **Hound glove:** These gloves actually slip over your hand. They are covered on one side with natural bristles. Rub these gloves over your smooth-coated dog to remove dead hair efficiently, brightening and shining the coat.
- **Mat comb/mat splitter/coat rake:** These "combs" are specifically designed to remove mats in long and curly coats. They break up matted hair with angled teeth and work best in conjunction with a spray or liquid detangling product. There is a more detailed discussion of how to get rid of mats later in the book.
- **Natural bristle brush:** This brush has bristles that are softer, gentler, and less likely to cause static electricity in a dog's coat than artificial

you may require for your breed. Review the notes on which brushes and combs your breed's coat type requires to be sure that you have the tools you need.

Many brushes and combs can substitute for other types, especially if you are not grooming for the show ring. A pin brush can take the place of a slicker brush in some breeds. A hound glove can take the place of a curry comb. However, to best use each tool for its specific purpose, the following is a brief description of what each kind of brush and comb is really meant to do.

- **Fine/medium/wide-toothed combs:** Fine and medium combs are best for dogs with soft, silky, fine- to medium-textured hair. They work through the coat to remove any last traces of tangle, and they also double as flea combs to help remove parasites and flea dirt when present. Wide-toothed combs are better for breeds with very thick, dense coats, but they

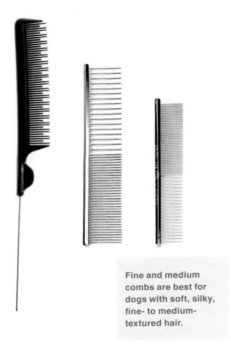

Fine and medium combs are best for dogs with soft, silky, fine- to medium-textured hair.

bristles, such as those made from nylon. Natural bristle brushes are all-purpose brushes designed to smooth hair and distribute natural oils in the coat.

- Pin brush: Pin brushes are generally used for longhaired breeds like Shih Tzu and Lhasa Apsos and heavily double-coated breeds like Old English Sheepdogs and Chow Chows. Pin brushes help detangle long, tangle-prone coats and also work well on hard wire coats for an overall brushing prior to hand-stripping.
- Slicker brush: The slicker brush has densely set wire teeth effective at removing mats and dead coat from long-, wire-, and curly-coated dogs. Slicker brushes are great when your dog is blowing (shedding) his coat because they efficiently remove large amounts of dead hair. But because they can also pull out some of the live hair, they aren't ideal for show dogs who

want to maintain luxurious coats. They are ideal for grooming heavy shedders around the house, however, as they get rid of maximum amounts of hair with minimum effort.

- Rubber curry brush: These oval-shaped rubber brushes are perfect for smooth coats because they polish the coat and remove dead hair, minimizing shedding, but the rounded rubber "bristles" are gentle on the sensitive skin of smooth-coated breeds.

BRUSH YOUR DOG STEP BY STEP

Brushing out your dog before a bath can be time consuming or quick, depending on coat type and condition. Although it doesn't really matter which parts of your dog you brush in what order (as long as you cover the whole coat), an orderly and systematic brush-out from front to back and bottom to top will ensure that you cover all parts of your dog. It will also reassure him that you will always groom the same way, so he'll know exactly what to expect. In long-coated dogs and long curly-coated dogs especially, brushing (and combing) takes a long time and a lot of patience. Having a routine can be reassuring to your dog, especially before he is entirely accustomed to the process.

Brush and then comb each section before moving on to the next section. In dogs with smooth coats, brushing is sufficient unless you are combing through the coat to remove fleas. Feel free to vary this order, but try to remain consistent. Many groomers find that brush-outs work best if they follow this sequence. Call it your 12-step grooming program.

1.) Back Legs

First, begin at your dog's back legs. Brush down each leg with a natural bristle brush for smooth and medium coats and a pin brush or slicker brush for long, wire, and curly coats. If you encounter tangles or mats, hold the hair at the root as you work out the tangle with the slicker brush or with a mat comb. (There are specific instructions on using a mat comb to remove a mat in Chapter 15.) Holding the hair above the tangle will minimize discomfort to your dog because you won't be yanking at the skin.

Once the back legs are completely free of tangles and mats, finish with a comb. The comb should run smoothly through the hair from root to end. In smooth coats, a comb can ensure that your dog is parasite-free even if it is unnecessary as a detangler. Don't worry about trimming paw hair or nails just yet. You can put these finishing touches on your dog after the bath.

2.) Front Legs

Next, move to the front legs. Again, work from the top of each leg to the bottom, first brushing the coat, then removing tangles and mats one at a time, then working through the coat a final time with a comb.

3.) Tail

Back to the rear again, brush out your dog's tail (if he has one) from base to tip, covering top, sides, and bottom. Even a smooth-coated tail can use a good brushing to remove dead hair, but many breeds have a feathered tail, and this must be kept brushed and combed to stay mat-free, especially at the base, where hair can tangle against the rear end. If your dog doesn't have a tail or has a short, docked tail, brush what is there.

4.) Hindquarters

After brushing the tail, turn your attention to your dog's hindquarters. Many

> **Brush and then comb each section of your dog completely before moving on to the next section.**

breeds have thicker furnishings in this area. Brush out feathers, "pantaloons," or the smooth haunches of your dog, slowly working out tangles in long coats. When cutting a tangle, cut in the direction the hair grows, and split the tangle with scissors. Then use a brush or comb to work the tangle free.

Brush carefully around the anal area, checking for mats and ensuring that your dog's rear end is clean and free of soil. Be careful not to brush over sensitive skin. Using blunt-tipped scissors, trim off any tangles that are unworkable and any soil stuck in long hair. For extra cleanliness, shave just around the anal area with clippers (but never directly over the anal area) or trim closely with blunt-tipped scissors.

Finally, comb the hindquarters to check one more time that this area is tangle-free.

5.) Back

Next, brush down your dog's back, from nape to tail base. Or in long-coated dogs, begin at the base of

the tail and work through sections of hair, brushing out tangles and mats as you go. Follow with a comb on each section until the entire back is tangle-free.

6.) Sides

Brush your dog along each side from nape to tail base. Again, in long-coated dogs, begin at the base of the tail and work through sections of hair. In dogs with shorter coats, you can brush the back and sides together with long, firm strokes to stimulate skin and distribute natural oils in the coat.

7.) Belly

Now it's time to do your dog's underside. In many dogs, the belly has little hair, but check it over and brush lightly to prevent brush burn on your dog's sensitive underside. Don't brush areas without hair or with more skin showing than hair.

8.) Chest

With your dog in the *sit* position, brush the chest, working out tangles.

9.) Neck

Many dogs have longer, thicker coats around the neck area, called a "ruff" in some breeds. Get all the way down to the skin with the brush and then with the comb to make sure that no hidden tangles remain in the ruff's undercoat.

Brush Up On a Breed

Breeds that need special attention to the long hair on their ears include the following:

- Afghan Hound
- American Water Spaniel
- Bearded Collie
- Bedlington Terrier
- Bernese Mountain Dog
- Bichon Frise
- Briard
- Cavalier King Charles Spaniel
- Chinese Crested
- Cocker Spaniel
- Dachshund (Longhaired)
- Dandie Dinmont Terrier
- English Cocker Spaniel
- English Setter
- English Springer Spaniel
- English Toy Spaniel
- Field Spaniel
- Gordon Setter
- Irish Setter
- Irish Water Spaniel
- Japanese Chin
- Lhasa Apso
- Löwchen
- Maltese
- Old English Sheepdog
- Otterhound
- Papillon
- Pekingese
- Petit Basset Griffon Vendeen
- Polish Lowland Sheepdog
- Poodle (all sizes)
- Portuguese Water Dog
- Puli
- Saluki
- Shih Tzu
- Skye Terrier
- Sussex Spaniel
- Tibetan Terrier
- Yorkshire Terrier

Feathered tails must be kept brushed and combed to prevent mats.

10.) Ears

If your dog has long ear hair, spend time brushing and combing the ears carefully and gently. Beautifully combed ears make a big difference in the overall appearance of a longhaired dog (or a long-ear-haired dog!). Work out tangles gently, as many dogs have sensitive ears.

11.) Head

Gently brush your dog's head and finish with a comb. In smooth-coated dogs, a rubdown with a hound glove is enough.

12.) Face

If your dog has long facial hair, brush and comb it carefully, trimming as necessary and appropriate for your breed. In smooth-coated dogs, simply wipe down the face with a moist, soft cloth.

Ask the Groomer

Q: Is grooming a chore that my kids can help with?

A: Kids love dogs, and involving your child in daily grooming is a great way to foster this relationship, teaching her that dogs need care and teaching dogs that a child can care for them gently and responsibly. When your child is old enough to follow directions and be gentle (this could be anywhere from age 4 to age 12, depending on your child's personality), teach her how to use brushes and combs on your dog's coat. Always supervise grooming sessions!

THE BATH

Giving a dog a bath can be as simple as rinsing him down in a child's swimming pool in the backyard during the summer or as complex as a full-blown spa ritual, complete with bathing harness and a bevy of fancy coat products designed to whiten, darken, brighten, detangle, shine, or leave your dog with a designer aroma to rival a fancy French perfume. However, there are many ways to make bathing easier and many ways in which bathing makes subsequent grooming sessions easier too. In this chapter, we'll show you how to give your dog a bath that makes a difference—one that will facilitate grooming and be easy and as pleasant as possible for your dog.

TAKE INVENTORY

Once your dog is completely brushed, combed, and tangle-free, he is ready for a bath. Now you must get ready too, and that means preparing all the necessary equipment and supplies so that you can reach what you need when you need it. If you put your dog in the bathtub under running water and then have to go in search of shampoo or a scrub brush, we all know what will happen: a jump, a shake, and you will be left with a soaked bathroom and a wet dog bounding around the house.

To wash your dog, you will need some basic supplies at hand:

- bath mat
- conditioner
- dog shampoo (not made for humans)
- handheld sprayer or a large plastic cup for rinsing
- heavy towel (or two)

Before bathing your dog, gather together all the supplies you will need.

- nylon collar and leash, if you think that your dog is likely to bolt or will be difficult to hang on to in the bath
- plastic or rubber apron for you (or wear clothes that can get wet—some precautionary pet owners don a bathing suit for this job)
- scrub brush
- small scrub brush or soft-bristled nail brush (for the face)
- sponge

Assemble your supplies, then place them within easy reach of the sink or tub where you will bathe your dog.

CHOOSE A SHAMPOO

With so many shampoos on the market, it's not easy to decide which to use. Yet for most breeds, a basic, all-purpose dog shampoo is fine. If you want your shampoo to do more than clean, you might also consider a specialty shampoo:

- Accentuate your dog's coat color by choosing a shampoo made for white, black, or red coats.
- Shampoos designed to deliver extra conditioning to long or curly coats can make post-bath grooming even easier.
- For wire-coated dogs, look for a shampoo designed to preserve the crisp texture of your dog's coat.
- Many dogs have sensitive skin or eyes. A hypoallergenic shampoo can minimize sensitivity reactions to bathing.
- If your dog already has a rash, allergies, itching, or other sensitive skin conditions, look for a medicated shampoo designed to treat his problem. (Your vet should be able to recommend a good medicated shampoo.)
- Flea season? Consider a shampoo containing a gentle anti-flea ingredient such as pyrethrin or limonene or any of several natural botanicals that repel fleas, such as neem oil.
- Sensitive eyes? Consider a tearless shampoo.

DECIDE ON LOCATION

But where will you bathe your dog? First, consider his size. While you can bathe a Yorkie in a clean kitchen sink, your Labrador Retriever isn't going to fit. Your Great Dane may outsize your bathtub, but your Chihuahua might be hard to hold onto all the way down in that big tub.

Size matters when it comes to bathing, and so does coat type. Long and curly coats need more time and attention in the bath, and if you are stooping or kneeling uncomfortably, you may not be able to spend as much time as you should washing and conditioning your dog's coat.

Bathing Small Breeds

In general, consider bathing small dogs in a kitchen or bathroom sink. If your sink doesn't come equipped with a drain that will trap hair, purchase a simple, inexpensive one that sits over the drain. Make sure that the sink is clean and your counter is uncluttered. You don't want to try to bathe a dog

Kitchen sinks are good for bathing small dogs because the dogs are easy to reach and rinse.

amidst piles of dirty dishes!

Kitchen sinks are good for bathing small dogs, especially when they come equipped with sprayers, because the dogs are easy to reach and easy to rinse. If you keep both your kitchen and your dog squeaky clean, you won't have to worry about contaminating your food preparation area. Just spray with a disinfectant and wipe down the counters and sink when you are done. Plus, you'll have a better time holding onto your small dog if you don't have to kneel on a hard tile floor.

If you can't quite get yourself to bathe your dog in the kitchen, consider the bathroom sink basin or the laundry tub. You can always purchase a spray attachment. Some bathroom sinks have faucets that aren't compatible with sprayers, and if yours isn't, look for one with a long enough hose that you can attach it to the bathtub faucet or showerhead and stretch it over to the sink.

Bathing Medium-Sized Breeds

Medium-sized breeds are too big for a kitchen sink but will fit nicely in your bathtub or a laundry tub. Dogs from approximately 15 to 50 pounds (7 to 22.5 kg) are easy to bathe in a regular bathtub. Fold a towel on the floor to make kneeling more comfortable. Invest in a good sprayer, and put a bath mat on the tub floor so that your dog doesn't slip and slide. A hose diverter for the shower connection can be installed between the showerhead and pipe and will make bathing much easier.

If kneeling beside the tub is a problem, booster tubs can be purchased at a reasonable price. Water hookups and drainage can be near a bathtub or laundry area.

Bathing Large Breeds

You can bathe large breeds in your bathtub or shower too, but if your dog is large enough to step in and out of the bathtub without blinking an eye, remember that a good shake of that coat will spray water far and wide. This can be avoided by stepping into the shower with your dog and closing the shower curtain. Some pet owners like to bathe their larger dogs outside in a child's swimming pool or other large basin or simply by using the garden hose, if your dog doesn't mind the cold water.

BATHE YOUR DOG STEP BY STEP

You have your location, you have your supplies, and you are properly suited up for the likelihood of getting wet. Now it's time to transform that nicely brushed and combed dog into a squeaky *clean* dog.

If your dog isn't yet trained to stand nicely for bathing, put a nylon,

Waterproofing Your Dog

Well-behaved bathers won't struggle and probably won't get soap and water in their ears and eyes, but before you know for sure how well your dog will respond to a bath, protect those sensitive eyes and ears before getting him wet. Even a tear-free shampoo can irritate his eyes, so put a drop of mineral oil in the corner of each eye to repel water. Also, protect your dog's ears from getting wet, as a damp ear canal can encourage infection. Dip two cotton balls in a little petroleum jelly and insert in each ear to protect the ear canal. You can also hold the ears flat against the head to prevent water from entering the ear canal.

A basic, all-purpose dog shampoo is fine for most breeds.

You can bathe medium and large breeds in your bathtub.

plain buckle collar on him and attach a nylon leash. Loop this around a secure fixture, such as a shower railing, or attach the leash to your belt or wrist. Tub restraints with suction cups work well for holding smaller breeds. Once your dog is used to bathing, you may not have to do this, but some dogs will always try to escape the water, and some kind of precautionary restraint may necessarily become a part of the bathing routine. A leash and collar can actually make your dog feel more secure in the bathtub, and he may prefer them. Very important: Do not use any kind of choke collar or any material that will swell when wet to restrain your dog when bathing!

Bathing your dog in the same sequence each time can make the bath experience more comfortable because he will know exactly what to expect.

1.) Wet Down Your Dog

First, wet down your dog. Always test the water before applying it to him. Lukewarm water of approximately 110°F (43.3°C) is ideal. Depending on your dog's coat thickness and water-repellant qualities, this can take a few seconds or a couple of minutes of heavy soaking. (Double coats and curly coats tend to repel water.) Make sure that your dog is wet all the way down to the skin.

As with brushing, you can wet heavy, long coats according to a sequence. Start from the back and work your way to the front, saturating the hindquarters, body, front, and then carefully, the head, avoiding the eyes and ear canals. Move slowly and talk encouragingly to your dog so that he doesn't associate the experience with discomfort or fear.

2.) Soap Him Up

Once your dog's coat is completely saturated, apply shampoo according to the bottle's instructions. Generally, the more coat you have to cover, the more shampoo you will need. Grab that sponge and work the shampoo into a lather (or use your hands if you prefer—better exercise but you may generate less lather). Completely cover your dog with suds except for the face, which you can do at the end.

3.) Work It In

Now grab the scrub brush and gently scrub the soap all the way to the skin, massaging the skin and distributing the shampoo evenly over the coat. You can also work the lather in with your fingers,

Bathing your dog in the same sequence each time can make the bath experience more comfortable because he will know exactly what to expect.

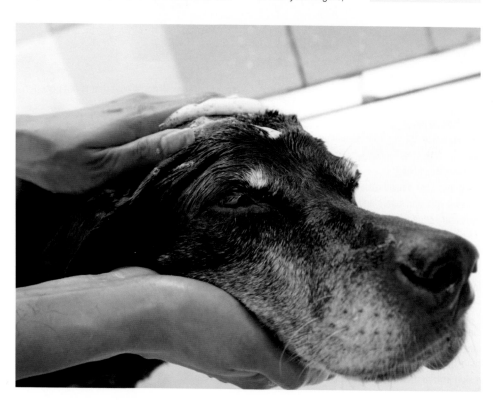

allowing you to feel your dog's skin for any unusual lumps or bumps. He will probably enjoy this part—it should feel

After using shampoo, rinse the coat until the rinse water runs completely clear.

great. Use your small brush or nail brush to gently suds up your dog's ears and face, avoiding the eyes and ear canals.

4.) Rinse It Out

Now, using your handheld sprayer or plastic container, rinse his coat of all signs of soap. Long, heavy, and double coats may take a while. Keep rinsing until the rinse water runs completely clear. Even smooth coats may need to be rinsed a couple of times. Rinsing will probably take longer than sudsing. Soap left in your dog's coat can be a skin irritant and will compromise the look and feel of his coat. A dog's coat that is not rinsed properly will appear dull and flaky.

5.) Condition

Next, apply a conditioner or cream rinse after rinsing shampoo from the coat. Follow the package directions and rinse well. A conditioner will keep hair soft and manageable but may be overkill for smooth coats and could compromise the harsh texture of wire coats, so reserve conditioners/cream rinses for medium-, long-, and curly-coated breeds.

6.) Dry

Finally, dry your dog's coat. Ring as much water out of the coat with your hands as you can, either by squeezing or by running your palm along the coat like a squeegee. Then dry as much of his coat as you can with a heavy towel.

Wet dogs have an automatic impulse to shake, and even if you think that you have dried your dog pretty well, you'll probably feel a fine spray when he shakes himself after you remove him from the tub or sink. After that efficient shake, smooth-coated dogs usually don't need any more drying, but you aren't finished with your grooming session, so don't let your dog bound along on his merry way just yet.

For thicker and longer-coated dogs, blow-drying will dry the coat more quickly and it will put it into good shape for clipping and styling, if appropriate for your breed. Use a cool or warm setting on your dog, constantly monitoring the blow-dryer temperature to make sure that it doesn't get too hot.

For long or curly coats, blow-dry a section at a time, brushing or combing and fluffing lightly and quickly as you go, depending on coat type and desired appearance. For straight coats, dry quickly in sections to avoid kinks and waves, brushing out each section briskly to keep it smooth. If some parts of the coat dry too quickly and kink up, re-wet them and blow-dry straight. Some curly coats can benefit from a diffuser to keep the curl in the coat. Other curly coats should be brushed out, depending on the breed and style. (For more on blow-drying long and curly coats, see the appropriate chapters in Part Three.)

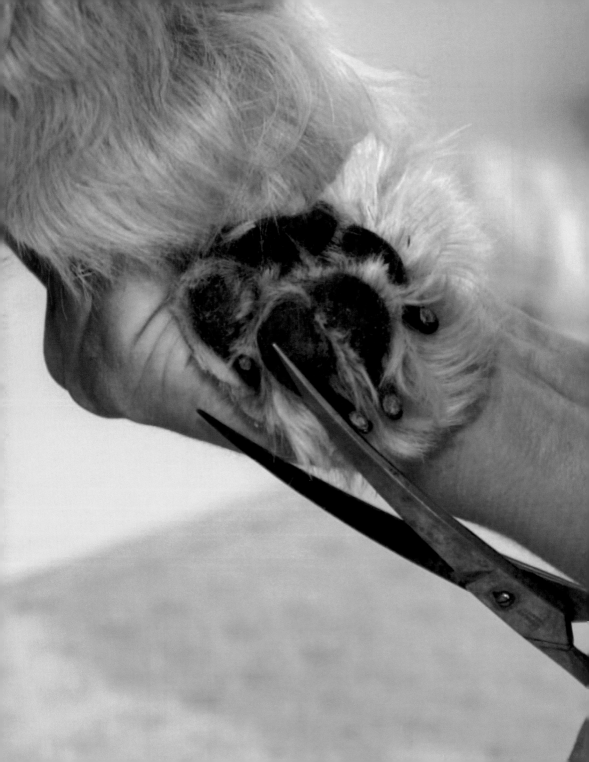

6

THE DOGGY MANICURE

Take a look at those paws. Are your dog's nails neatly trimmed and short, or are they long, curving out from his paws and causing his paw pads to spread out when he takes a step? Nail trimming is essential not only for keeping the feet neat but also for preserving correct mobility, and ultimately, orthopedic health. Your dog can't walk or run correctly and comfortably if his nails are too long.

START EARLY

Some pet owners claim that their pets absolutely *hate* nail trimming—that the process is a horrible struggle or virtually impossible. Some give up and take their pets to a groomer to do the job. But nail trimming doesn't have to be a bad experience for dog and human alike. Trimming your dog's nails is easy if he is well trained to tolerate the practice. Many dogs don't like it—some breeds more than others—but those dogs whose nails were trimmed every week or two from puppyhood usually don't bat an eye at the procedure.

Begin trimming your new puppy's nails the very first week you bring him home. Handle his paw pads frequently, and make it rewarding. Wiggle each nail and press on each paw pad, then always offer lots of praise, petting, and a treat. Do this every day for the first few months of your puppy's life to teach him that when a human touches his feet, good things happen.

After a week of paw play, let your puppy investigate the nail trimmer in the presence of rewards. Let him sniff it. Don't just pull it out and start clipping, or you could scare your puppy. Once your puppy has had a chance to investigate the nail trimmers, take them in your hand, take your puppy's paw, and carefully clip off just the very tip of the nail. Immediately reward him. If he responds well, try another nail and reward again. (A pocketful of tiny pieces of cheese, treats, or kibble—no larger than a fingernail—works well for most puppies.)

Keep the process fun and always clip off just a tiny bit of nail. One slip, resulting in clipping the puppy's nail vein (or "quick") and you could set back nail trimming for months. This is because

Training your dog to accept nail trimming as a puppy will make the job much easier when he is an adult.

clipping the quick hurts, and the nail will bleed. Be careful. Keep handling your puppy's paws, clip the nails weekly, and continue to give treats, and your puppy will soon learn that nail trimming is something rewarding, not something uncomfortable or scary.

This type of early training will also teach your dog exactly what those nail trimmers are about and exactly what to expect. Just like anything else in your dog's life, routines, especially those routines that begin in puppyhood, become comforting and familiar. If a weekly toenail trim has always been part of your dog's life, the job should be an easy one.

TRIM OFTEN

Weekly? Does your dog really need a weekly toe trim? Weekly trims are especially good for dogs who are always on carpets or grass because their nails are not worn down naturally. Actually, a monthly toe trim would be perfectly appropriate for most dogs, but a month is about the longest most dog owners should wait before trimming nails. However, trimming weekly has some real benefits.

• Weekly toenail trims involve only the clip of the toenail's tip. Monthly trims require cutting off more nail.

The Concrete Manicure

Dogs who are walked daily on hard surfaces or dogs who spend a lot of time on cement, stones, or other hard surfaces may not need their nails trimmed as often because the cement will naturally wear down the nail surface. Dogs who spend most of their time on grass or carpet will need more frequent nail trimming.

Beauty Tip

Some dogs retain their dewclaws: vestigial toes higher up on the leg with nails attached. These nails must also be clipped regularly, or they can grow so long that they curve back around and pierce the skin. Keep an eye—and the trimmers—on the dewclaws if your dog didn't have them removed in puppyhood.

• Weekly toenail trims encourage the quick—that vein that runs down each nail—to recede so that you can clip nails shorter without risking the bleeding associated with accidentally clipping the quick.

• Weekly toenail trims are more routine than monthly toenail trims, so your dog will get used to them more quickly.

• Weekly toenail trims are so quick and easy that they are much less stressful on your pet. These short sessions, especially when followed by lots of praise and perhaps a tasty treat, will quickly become pleasant and rewarding for your dog.

TRIM THE NAILS STEP BY STEP

Nail trimming should be part of your monthly grooming routine. You can trim your dog's nails first, after brushing, or just after your dog has been washed and dried. Trimming nails after the bath may be the easiest, especially for large dogs with thick nails, because bathing helps soften the nails.

1.) Prepare Your Tools

Assemble the following:

• baby oil
• nail file or nail grinder/dremel tool
• nail trimmers

- styptic pencil or styptic powder, silver nitrate stick, or other coagulant in case of bleeding
- treats (no larger than a fingernail)

> Trimming the nails after a bath may be easiest because bathing helps soften them.

2.) Situate Your Dog

Next, prepare your dog by having him sit on the grooming table or the ground in front of you, facing you. If he is larger, have him stand on the floor. Stand or kneel next to him, facing the opposite direction, so that you can lift up each paw behind him to clip it. (Stand or kneel on the right as you do the right paws, and move to the left to do the left paws.)

3.) Clip the Nails

Take one of your dog's paws gently in your left hand. Take the nail clipper in your right hand (or switch if you are left handed).

Hold the clipper blade parallel with the plane of your dog's paw and clip off the tip of the nail, just below the quick.

If your dog is comfortable lying on his back, you can sit on the floor and have him between your legs with his head at your feet. This way your dog's paw pads will be facing you and you can see the underside of the toenail. Give him a treat and a belly rub after each clip of a nail.

Brush Up On a Breed

Some breeds in particular, such as the Yorkshire Terrier, have a bit of hair that grows between the paw pads. Take the time to trim this hair after clipping the nails because if you don't, the hair can mat and even cause your dog to lose his footing.

4.) Smooth the Nails

With the file or grinder/dremel tool, smooth down the rough nail. Train sensitive dogs not to fear the electric tool by introducing it to them a little at a time: At first, introduce the tool itself; next, the tool turned on but not touching the dog; and finally, tiny bits of touching the paw at a time. Reward your dog's brave investigation of the tool throughout the process with lots of praise and treats.

5.) Polish and Shine

For extra polish and shine, rub a tiny bit of baby oil on each nail and on the paw pads to keep them moist. Don't rub on too much, however, as it will make your dog's feet slippery. Or instead of a drop of oil, give your pampered pooch a dash of color with nail polish made just for dogs.

Nail trimming should be part of your monthly grooming routine.

Ask the Groomer

Q: How do I find the quick in my dog's nails?

A: If your dog has light nails, you should be able to see the quick, the darker vein running down the middle of the nail. In dark-nailed dogs, you probably won't be able to see the quick and are best off clipping just the tip weekly. If you do clip the quick or grind down to it with an electric tool, your dog will feel pain and the quick will bleed, sometimes profusely. You'll need to stop the bleeding with the styptic pencil, styptic powder, silver nitrate stick, or other coagulant. Apply pressure and then the coagulant.

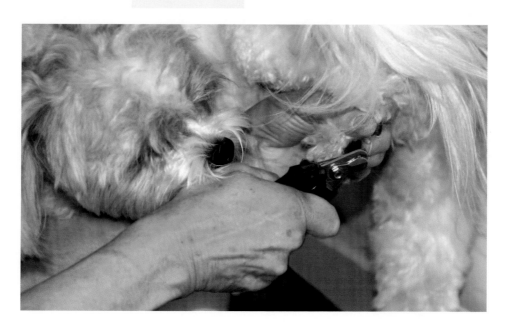

7

EYES, EARS, TEETH, AND REARS

Now that your dog is brushed, washed, dried, and has had his toenails clipped, you just have a few more things to do to complete the monthly grooming routine: Give his eyes, ears, teeth, and rear the once-over.

These areas of your dog's body all require proper hygiene, maintenance, and attention. Neglected eyes, ears, teeth, and rears can all become unsightly and even infected, so do your dog a favor and keep these areas well maintained. You can save a lot of money on vet care, not to mention avoiding pain and suffering for your dog.

You will need these tools and products for this portion of the monthly grooming session:

- cotton balls
- dental scaler, for heavy plaque deposits
- ear hair tweezers and/or small scissors
- ear powder
- earwash or mineral oil
- heavy gauze for emptying anal glands, if necessary
- moisturizing eye drops (for dogs with dry eyes) or canine eyewash
- small spray bottle
- tearstain remover (for light-colored dogs, if tearstains are a problem)
- toothbrush or a piece of gauze big enough to wrap around your finger
- toothpaste made for dogs

THE EYES HAVE IT

First, take a good look at your dog's eyes. Depending on the breed, the eyes may be receded, narrow, almond shaped, almost round, or round and slightly protruding. Different eye types need different kinds of care.

- The protruding eyes of brachycephalic, or flat-faced, dogs require the most care because they are less protected than eyes that are set deeper and protected by a long muzzle. They dry out easily and are easily injured.
- Dogs with white fur may develop tearstains—brownish streaks under the eyes.
- Dogs with entropion, a condition in which the lid turns inward and eyelashes irritate the cornea, need special attention, and in extreme cases, surgery to correct the problem.

A doggy toothbrush and toothpaste are essential grooming supplies.

- Dogs with excessive tearing need the eye area to be kept clean and dry.
- Dogs with dry eyes require moisturizing eye drops every day.

Check your dog's eyes every day, not just monthly.

1.) Check the Eyes Daily

Check your dog's eyes every day, not just monthly. First make sure that the eyes are clear; cloudiness could mean that he is developing cataracts. Most dogs occasionally accumulate debris in the corners of their eyes, and they will benefit from wiping the face down with a moist cloth and cleaning the corners of the eyes with a moist cotton ball every day. (Don't wipe the cotton ball over the eye or you could scratch the cornea.)

Many dogs with protruding eyes require a daily dose of moisturizing eye drops to keep their eyes moist and comfortable. (Some brands of human eye drops work, but check with your vet about

Brush Up On a Breed

Always be careful of your dog's eyes during grooming, especially if he has protruding eyes, like the Pug or Chihuahua. Scissors, clippers, and even brushes and combs could seriously injure an eye if you aren't paying attention. Always have the points of scissors or the edges of clippers pointing away from the eyes. Try to use blunt-tipped scissors near the eyes and ears.

which brand to use.) If you check, clean, and moisturize your dog's eyes every day, he will soon get used to the ritual.

If your light-coated dog has tearstains, be very diligent about wiping the eyes clean daily, and apply a tearstain remover to the stained fur (not to the eyes themselves) according to the directions for the individual product.

2.) Wash Eyes Monthly

During monthly sessions, rinse your dog's eyes with canine eyewash or eye drops. Put a drop in each eye and carefully wipe away excess from the corners with a soft cloth or dry cotton ball.

3.) Get a Yearly Vet Exam

Finally, a yearly vet exam is crucial to keeping eyes healthy, and your vet can help detect eye diseases in the early stages so that they can best be treated.

EAR YE, EAR YE

Whether your dog's ears are long and droopy or short and cat-like, they require attention. Ears produce wax, trap dirt, grow hair, retain moisture,

Ask the Groomer

Q: My dog's eyes always seem to be tearing up. What should I do?

A: If your dog seems to be tearing excessively, so that even when you wipe his eyes clean every day he is still constantly wet under the eyes, or if you notice unusual redness or swollen areas in or around the eye, consult your vet. Dogs can develop many different minor eye disorders that are easily treated.

Treats and Toys for Better Teeth

Dogs who eat hard, crunchy dog biscuits and hard kibble enjoy the benefits of natural teeth cleaning from these treats. (Choose treats made with natural ingredients and low in preservatives if you can.) Avoid feeding soft, unhealthy "people food." Many dog toys are also designed specifically to clean teeth, so let your dog enjoy these as well. But don't let biscuits and toys do the whole job. For the best dental care, you should still brush and check your dog's teeth at least once a week and ideally every day.

and can easily develop infections when they aren't kept clean, plucked, and dry.

Check your dog's ears every day. If he is used to ear handling, he will be more comfortable with it when a professional groomer or vet has to touch his ears. Then during the monthly grooming session, spend a little more time on those ears.

1.) Examine the Ears

First, examine your dog's ears. Check the outside for tangles and parasites, which often gravitate toward the ears. Inspect the insides for dirt and excessive wax buildup. Your dog's ears should be clean. A little earwax is normal, but ask your vet about large amounts or about earwax that looks reddish brown or streaky or smells funny.

2.) Check for Hair

Next, check for hair inside the ear. Ear hair can trap dirt, bacteria, and moisture inside the ear canal, causing infection. Trimming ear hair also makes the ears appear neater and more attractive.

To trim ear hair, first pull the ear back over the dog's head, laying it flat against the skull. This will shut off the delicate parts of the ear canal. For long ear hair, pluck out individual hairs with your fingers. If you find this difficult, dip your fingers in a little ear powder to make it easier to grasp them. Don't pluck out more than two hairs at one time, as this could be painful to your dog. Use ear hair forceps—small tweezers made for plucking ear hair. Again, only pluck one or two hairs at a time. For shorter hair that is hard to pluck, or if you prefer to cut rather than pluck, clip ear hair with small, blunt-tipped scissors.

For drop-eared dogs, keep all hair under the ear opening and on the inside flap of the ear trimmed short. This will increase airflow to the ear and reduce the likelihood of ear infections.

3.) Dust With Medicated Powder

Dust the ears with medicated ear powder if they are prone to infection.

4.) Clean With Earwash

If the ears are very dirty, gently pull them out away from the skull to open up the ear canal and place a few drops of earwash or mineral oil in the ear. Massage the base of the ear to work the cleanser down into the canal. Hold the ear down for a minute to let the fluid enter the canal, then release

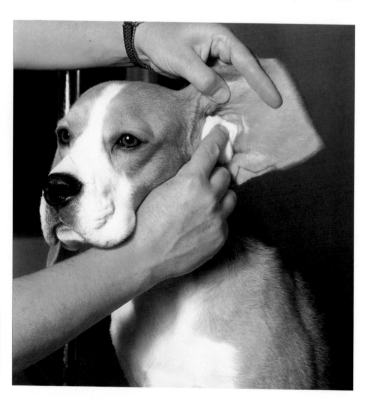

Clean loosened wax from your dog's ear with a cotton ball dipped in earwash or mineral oil.

your dog and let him shake his head a few times to loosen any earwax. Check the ears again and clean out loosened wax with a cotton ball dipped in earwash or mineral oil.

THOSE PEARLY WHITES

Dog teeth may be longer and sharper than human teeth, but they develop plaque and tartar in the same way we do. When the clear, sticky plaque film isn't brushed away, it hardens and develops into ugly brown tartar that can compromise gum integrity and result in infection. Oral infections are particularly dangerous because they can quickly travel to the heart, and more than a few dogs have become extremely ill (or worse) due to neglected dental care.

1.) Check for Tartar

You can tell when your dog has tartar buildup: Tartar is the hard brown stuff that sticks to your dog's teeth, and you can't just brush it away. It must be scraped with a dental scaler. Some people like to try this themselves; others leave the job to their vets. You can prevent tartar buildup by keeping your dog's teeth cleaned of plaque. Don't wait until the monthly grooming session to brush your dog's teeth!

2.) Brush the Teeth

Brush the teeth at least once a week, or even better, once a day as part of the daily grooming session. Keep those pearly whites…well, pearly white!

Brush your dog's teeth at least once a week, but ideally, you should brush them daily.

Some dogs don't mind having their teeth brushed, but others rebel against the process and need to be introduced to the tools and methods of dental care gradually and with lots of rewards. Here's how to do this:

1. First, let your dog sniff the toothbrush and lick some of the toothpaste off your finger. Praise him for investigating.

2. The next day, let him sniff the toothbrush again and touch it against his muzzle. Praise and reward your dog with a treat. If he doesn't like the taste of doggy toothpaste, don't worry—the point isn't to eat it. The point is to get your dog used to the taste of the toothpaste and to the feel of the brush.

3. The next day, speaking calmly and reassuringly to your dog, take his muzzle in your hand and part his lips along the side. Touch the brush to his teeth, then immediately praise and reward him.

4. On the following day, rub the brush against his teeth for just a few seconds. Praise and reward. If at any point during this process your dog gets nervous or scared, back up a step but don't give up.

5. Finally, put a little toothpaste on the toothbrush and rub it briefly on your dog's teeth. Brush his teeth for a slightly longer period each time you try it until he is so used to the process that he enjoys the attention. (Don't forget the lavish praise!)

Once your dog is used to having his teeth brushed, the following procedure will ensure that you do a good and thorough job. Here's how to brush his teeth step by step.

1. Using a soft toothbrush or one designed for dogs, put a small amount of toothpaste on the brush, or put toothpaste on a piece of gauze wrapped around your finger.

2. Open your dog's mouth, exposing his teeth, and brush both teeth and gums as you would brush your own teeth.

3. Make sure that you brush along the gum line, where plaque and tartar accumulate first. Don't press too hard or you could injure your dog's gums.

Beauty Tip

You can buy all kinds of toothbrush-inspired products designed to clean your dog's teeth, but all you really need is a regular soft toothbrush and toothpaste made for dogs. (Human toothpaste has ingredients that aren't healthy for your dog.) However, you can also buy bristled rubber fingertip toothbrushes that fit over your index finger, different sizes and shapes of toothbrushes, tooth-brushing sponges, dental sprays (like mouthwash for dogs), toys, and even breath fresheners.

4. Avoid any red, irritated, or infected-looking areas, and tell your vet about them.

5. If your dog has excessive tartar (most common on the top teeth), use the dental scraper to carefully scrape the teeth from just under the gum line to the tip. Protect the gums with your fingers, and be careful not to scrape the gums. Or make a vet appointment to have this done professionally, especially if tartar deposits are very heavy.

6. Spray your dog's mouth with water to rinse off the toothpaste and debris, and you're done!

3.) Look for Changes

On a monthly basis, do more than a cursory oral check. Look carefully for changes, tartar accumulation, loose teeth, and red areas that

Be sure to brush along the gum line, where plaque and tarter accumulate first.

could signal a gum infection. Let your vet know about any suspicious-looking changes. Remember, dental infections can travel straight to your dog's heart, so don't ignore them!

THE NOTORIOUS ANAL GLANDS

All dogs have anal glands located on either side of the rectum. These glands produce a pungent brown fluid and should empty naturally when your dog defecates. However, in many dogs, these glands become blocked or even impacted and must be emptied by hand. It's not a pretty job, but somebody has to do it!

1.) Decide Who's Going to Do It

Your dog may never need his anal glands emptied, but if yours does, you can pay your vet a lot of money to do it, you can beg and plead and bribe a professional groomer to do it, or you can do it yourself.

2.) Look for Signs the Glands Need Emptying

Dogs who are accustomed to lots of grooming-related handling may not mind this process, and dogs who are used to it don't mind it at all. In fact, it probably relieves some discomfort. Signs that your dog's anal glands need to be emptied include scooting along the floor or excessive licking of the area.

3.) Empty the Glands

The anal glands are located below the rectum at the four o'clock and eight o'clock positions. To empty them, first place a square of gauze over the rectum to catch the fluid, which will spurt or ooze out. Using your thumb and index finger, push out, down, and inward to empty the glands. You may need to try it a few times, but don't do so to the point of upsetting your dog. If you can't seem to do it, have your vet or groomer show you how. (It's worth paying for an office visit to get this instruction.)

If you empty the anal glands during a bath, it will be easy to rinse the fluid away. If you do so afterward or on a day when you aren't giving your dog a bath, catch the fluid with the gauze pad or expel the glands outside, then clean the area with a warm washcloth.

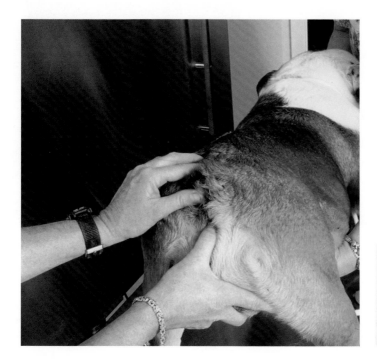

If your dog's anal glands need to be emptied and you're not sure what to do, have your vet or groomer show you how.

PART THREE

COAT-SPECIFIC

GROOMING GUIDE

8

GROOMING THE SMOOTH AND MEDIUM COATS

The smooth and medium coats are by far the easiest to groom. People who show dogs with smooth and medium coats in conformation shows often admit that they chose the dogs they now obsess about because they can "wash and go" from bathtub to show ring with virtually no effort at all. Many of these breeds are shown in a completely natural state. Others require only very small amounts of trimming here and there to neaten areas of longer or shaggier hair growth. In general, however, smooth and medium coats are the lazy groomer's dream.

owever easy to groom the shorter coats may be, you can do many things to make them look great. In this chapter, we will first discuss smooth coats and then medium coats, giving you some helpful hints and tricks for keeping these coats looking their best.

GROOMING THE SMOOTH COAT

First let's look at the smooth coat. Sleek, hard, glossy, and shape defining, the smooth coat is probably the easiest of all coat types to groom because beyond brushing and the occasional bath, they don't require anything at all—no clipping, no shaving, no trimming, no shaping, and not even a blow-dry! Some dogs have their whiskers trimmed or certain areas neatened with a clipper for the show ring, but these details aren't necessary for pets. The two best things you can do to keep the smooth coat shiny and healthy are to brush often and bathe seldomly.

Although you don't need to brush your smooth-coated dog every day, you certainly can. He will enjoy the feeling and the time spent with you. Plus you'll keep the skin stimulated, the oil distributed over the coat, and the coat free of shed hairs, dirt, and even parasites. In fact, daily brushing could keep some dogs completely flea-free without the use of chemicals all year long (depending on where you live, the flea population in your area, and how often your dog goes outside—see later chapters for more on parasite prevention and treatment).

The Smooth-Coated Breeds

As a review, listed here are the smooth-coated breeds. If your breed is in this list or if your mixed-breed dog has a smooth coat, use the instructions in this section.

- American Foxhound
- American Staffordshire Terrier
- Basenji
- Basset Hound
- Beagle

Smooth-coated dogs are the easiest of all to groom.

Brush Up On a Breed

In most cases, grooming smooth coats or medium coats will be about the same for all the breeds with these coat types. However, a few individuals have certain coat specifications related to dog showing. Because this is a book primarily for at-home pet groomers, we won't always go into breed specifics. Pet grooming on many breeds is virtually identical. For more on how to groom all of the individual breeds for the show ring, check out a breed-specific grooming book like *All-Breed Dog Grooming.* A list of these can be found in the Resources section in the back of this book, or check the breed club website for specific information.

- Black and Tan Coonhound
- Bloodhound
- Boston Terrier
- Boxer
- Bulldog
- Bullmastiff
- Bull Terrier
- Chihuahua (smooth)
- Chinese Crested (hairless)
- Chinese Shar-Pei
- Dachshund (Smooth)
- Dalmatian
- Doberman Pinscher
- English Foxhound
- French Bulldog
- German Shorthaired Pointer
- Great Dane
- Greater Swiss Mountain Dog
- Greyhound
- Harrier
- Ibizan Hound
- Italian Greyhound
- Jack and Parson Russell Terriers (smooth)
- Labrador Retriever
- Manchester Terrier (Toy and Standard)
- Mastiff
- Miniature Pinscher
- Pharoah Hound
- Pointer
- Pug
- Rhodesian Ridgeback
- Rottweiler
- Smooth Fox Terrier
- Staffordshire Bull Terrier
- Toy Fox Terrier
- Vizsla
- Weimaraner
- Whippet

Tools

The following are the core tools for grooming the smooth coat:

- chamois, flannel, silk, or velvet squares for polishing
- coat conditioner spray or baby oil
- hound glove
- natural bristle brush
- rubber curry brush

How to Do It

Once a day—or at least once a week—give your smooth-coated dog a good brushing:

1. Begin with a thorough rubdown with the hound glove.
2. Remove dead hair and dirt with the rubber curry brush.
3. Brush the coat smooth with the natural bristle brush.
4. Polish the coat with the fabric square.
5. For special occasions (or just to make your dog look extra shiny), lightly spray the coat with coat conditioner or put a few drops of baby oil in your palms, rub them together, and smooth over your dog's coat.

Instant beauty!

Ask the Groomer

Q: Why can't I bathe my smooth-coated dog frequently?

A: Smooth-coated breeds tend to have sensitive skin (although there are exceptions). Too-frequent bathing can deplete the natural oils that give smooth coats their characteristic sheen, so don't worry about bathing your smooth-coated dog more than a couple of times a year unless he gets really dirty, such as after a swim in a lake, a day hunting out in the field, or if he rolls in, gets into, or tangles with something smelly (like a dead animal, garbage, or a skunk).

What Your Smooth Coat Should Look Like

This photo gallery demonstrates what your well-groomed smooth-coated dog should look like.

American Foxhound

Coat: Close, hard hound coat.
Colors: All colors.
Grooming: Brush occasionally with a stiff brush. Bathe only if absolutely necessary.

American Staffordshire Terrier

Coat: Short, close, stiff, glossy.
Colors: All colors.
Grooming: Brush regularly with a firm-bristled brush. Bathe occasionally.

Basenji

Coat: Short, sleek, close, fine.
Colors: Brindle, chestnut red, black, tricolor; white markings.
Grooming: Sometimes grooms himself. Groom with a hound glove. Clean facial wrinkles.

Basset Hound

Coat: Hard, smooth, short, dense.
Colors: Generally tricolor or bicolor.
Grooming: Easy-care coat, but saggy skin and ears require a thorough going-over several times a week.

Beagle

Coat: Close, dense, hard, weatherproof.
Colors: Any hound color.
Grooming: Easy-care coat. Bathe occasionally.

Black and Tan Coonhound

Coat: Short, dense, smooth, fine, glossy.
Colors: Black with rich tan markings.
Grooming: Groom with a hound glove. Ears need regular attention.

Bloodhound

Coat: Short, smooth, close lying, weatherproof.
Colors: Black and tan, liver and tan, red; may have white markings.
Grooming: Easy-care coat. Facial wrinkles and droopy ears require require regular attention.

Boston Terrier

Coat: Short, smooth, bright, fine.
Colors: Black, brindle, seal; white markings.
Grooming: Groom with a fine brush and soft cloth. Facial wrinkles require regular attention.

Boxer

Coat: Short, hard, shiny, lies smooth and tight against body.
Colors: Fawn shades, brindle; may have white markings; black mask.
Grooming: Simple rubdown and soft bristle brush. Facial wrinkles and flews require extra attention.

Bulldog

Coat: Short, straight, flat, close, fine, smooth, glossy.
Colors: Brindle, piebald, red, fawn, fallow, white.
Grooming: Easy-care coat with soft brush. Facial wrinkles require regular attention.

Bullmastiff

Coat: Short, hard, dense, weather resistant, lying flat to body.
Colors: Brindle, fawn, red; may have white marking; black muzzle.
Grooming: Easy-care coat using a firm bristle brush. Facial wrinkles require regular attention.

Bull Terrier

Coat: Short, flat, harsh, glossy.
Color: White, although head markings permissible.
Grooming: Easy-care coat with a hound glove and soft bristle brush.

Chihuahua (smooth)

Coat: Soft, close, glossy; neck ruff.
Colors: Any color.
Grooming: Occasional brushing and wiping with a soft, damp cloth. Eyes should be kept clean and debris-free.

Chinese Crested (hairless)

Coat: Soft, silky, flowing hair on head, tail, feet.
Colors: Any color or combination of colors.
Grooming: Regular bathing and applications of oil or cream on the skin to keep it soft and supple.

Chinese Shar-Pei

Coat: Single, straight, harsh.
Colors: Solid colors and sable.
Grooming: Brush regularly. Facial wrinkles and body folds require regular attention.

Dachshund (Smooth)

Coat: Short, dense, shiny, smooth fitting.
Colors: One colored, two colored, dappled.
Grooming: Quick going-over with a hound glove, soft brush, and damp cloth. Long ears should be checked regularly.

Dalmatian

Coat: Short, sleek, glossy, hard, dense.
Colors: Pure white ground color with black or liver-colored spots.
Grooming: Brush and currycomb often.

Doberman Pinscher

Coat: Smooth, short, hard, thick, close lying.
Colors: Black, red, blue, fawn; rust markings.
Grooming: Soft brush and hound glove are all that are needed.

English Foxhound

Coat: Short, hard, glossy, dense, weatherproof.
Colors: Any recognized hound color and markings.
Grooming: Occasional brushing.

French Bulldog

Coat: Short, fine, smooth, glossy, soft.
Colors: Any color but black; black and white, black and tan, liver, mouse.
Grooming: Occasional brushing. Facial wrinkles require regular attention.

German Shorthaired Pointer

Coat: Outercoat short, rough, dense; undercoat dense, short.
Colors: Solid liver, liver and white spotted, liver and white spotted and ticked, liver and white ticked, liver roan.
Grooming: Rub the coat with a nubbed hound glove to remove dead hair and massage the skin.

Great Dane

Coat: Short, thick, glossy.
Colors: Brindle, fawn, blue, black, harlequin, mantle.
Grooming: Easy-care coat requires regular brushing with a hound glove.

Greater Swiss Mountain Dog

Coat: Outercoat medium-length, thick, dense; undercoat dense, short.
Colors: Black with rich rust and white markings.
Grooming: Brush once a week.

Greyhound

Coat: Short, smooth, firm, close lying.
Colors: Black, white, red, blue, fawn, fallow, brindle, or any of these colors broken with white.
Grooming: Occasional brushing and rub with a hound glove or currycomb.

Harrier
Coat: Short, hard, dense, glossy, weatherproof.
Colors: Any color.
Grooming: Occasional brushing or rubbing with a hound glove.

Ibizan Hound
Coat: Smooth variety is strong, hard, shiny, dense, rough; rough variety is wiry, hard, dense; may have beard, mustache.
Colors: White or red, solid or in any combination.
Grooming: Smooth has easy-care coat that requires quick going-over with hound glove; rough needs just occasional brushing.

Italian Greyhound
Coat: Short, fine, glossy, soft.
Colors: All colors and markings acceptable except for brindle and tan markings found on black and tan dogs.
Grooming: Simple wiping down with a soft cloth.

Jack and Parson Russell Terriers
Coat: Smooth.
Colors: White predominating with black and/or tan markings.
Grooming: Easy-care coats with regular brushing and combing.

Labrador Retriever

Coat: Outercoat is short, straight, dense; undercoat is soft, weather resistant.
Colors: Black, yellow, chocolate.
Grooming: Frequent brushing.

Manchester Terrier

Coat: Short, smooth, glossy, dense, tight.
Colors: Jet black and rich mahogany tan.
Grooming: Occasional brushing.

Mastiff

Coat: Outercoat is moderately short, straight, coarse; undercoat is short, dense, close lying.
Colors: Fawn, apricot, brindle.
Grooming: Occasional brushing. Facial wrinkles require regular attention.

Miniature Pinscher

Coat: Short, straight, dense, smooth, shiny, close.
Colors: Solid red, stag red, black with rust-red markings, chocolate with rust-red markings.
Grooming: Minimal brushing.

Pharaoh Hound

Coat: Short, glossy, ranging from fine and close to slightly harsh.
Colors: Tan, rich tan; white markings permitted.
Grooming: Occasional brushing.

Pointer

Coat: Short, smooth, dense, with a sheen.
Colors: Liver, lemon, black, orange, either self-colored, tricolored, or with white.
Grooming: Occasional brushing and going-over with a soft cloth. Long ears should be checked frequently.

Pug

Coat: Short, smooth, fine, soft, glossy.
Colors: Fawn, black; mask.
Grooming: Occasional brushing. Facial wrinkles require regular attention.

Rhodesian Ridgeback

Coat: Short, sleek, glossy, dense.
Colors: Light wheaten to red wheaten.
Grooming: Occasional brushing or going-over with a hound glove.

Rottweiler

Coat: Outercoat is medium length, straight, coarse, dense, flat lying; undercoat.
Colors: Black with rust to mahogany markings.
Grooming: Brush and comb regularly. Facial folds require regular attention.

Smooth Fox Terrier

Coat: Short, hard, dense, abundant, close lying.
Colors: All white or predominantly white with tan, black and tan, or black markings.
Grooming: Quick going-over with a hound glove.

Staffordshire Bull Terrier

Coat: Short, smooth, close.
Colors: Red, fawn, white, black, blue, or any of these colors with white; any shade of brindle; any shade of brindle with white.
Grooming: Occasional brushing with a grooming mitt.

Toy Fox Terrier

Coat: Short, straight, flat, hard, abundant, smooth, satiny; neck ruff.
Colors: Tricolor, white, chocolate, tan; white and tan; white and black.
Grooming: Occasional grooming with a hound glove.

Vizsla

Coat: Short, smooth, dense, close lying.
Colors: Shades of golden rust.
Grooming: Occasional grooming with a hound glove.

Weimaraner

Coat: Shorthaired has short, strong, dense, smooth-lying outercoat.
Colors: Solid color in shades of mouse gray to silver-gray.
Grooming: Occasional brushing or rubdown with a hound glove.

Whippet

Coat: Short, smooth, firm, close.
Colors: Immaterial.
Grooming: Occasional brushing or going-over with a hound glove.

GROOMING THE MEDIUM COAT

Also easy to groom, many medium-coated dogs should remain completely natural without trimming, clipping, or shaping. The medium coat doesn't mat, tangle, hold on to dirt, or require much attention at all beyond regular brushing and the occasional bath.

As a general guideline, you can make slight adjustments to improve the shape of your dog by trimming the head versus the body to balance an uneven dog, and attending to certain areas—such as clipping the neck, neatening the ears, and cleaning the face with an electric clipper—in accordance with established show grooming for your breed. Spaniels and retrievers need hair removed from beneath the ears to improve airflow, and any long hair on the feet should be trimmed, especially between

toe pads where mats form. The sporting spaniels have the top third of their ears trimmed with clippers or thinning shears. The ruff on a spaniel's neck can be trimmed to 1 inch (2.5 cm) above the breastbone and blended into the shoulders. The other breeds with medium coats require very little trimming.

When relevant, you can also make small adjustments in shaping the ruff, rear furnishings, and ear hair, but in general, leave your medium-coated breed in a natural state, only neatening stray hairs without actually changing the dog's outline. The basic rule for medium-coated dogs is to brush often to remove shed hair. Less grooming is more.

The Medium-Coated Breeds

As a reminder, here are the medium-coated breeds. If your breed is among them or if your mixed-breed dog has a medium coat, follow the instructions in this section.

- Akita
- Alaskan Malamute
- American Eskimo Dog
- Australian Cattle Dog
- Australian Shepherd
- Belgian Malinois
- Belgian Sheepdog
- Belgian Tervuren
- Bernese Mountain Dog
- Borzoi
- Border Collie

You can either towel-dry or blow-dry your medium-coated breed after his bath.

- Brittany
- Canaan Dog
- Cardigan Welsh Corgi
- Cavalier King Charles Spaniel
- Chesapeake Bay Retriever
- Clumber Spaniel
- Collie (smooth)
- English Springer Spaniel
- Field Spaniel
- Finnish Spitz
- Flat-Coated Retriever
- German Shepherd Dog
- Golden Retriever
- Great Pyrenees
- Kuvasz
- Norwegian Elkhound
- Pembroke Welsh Corgi
- Saint Bernard
- Saluki
- Schipperke

The basic rule for medium-coated dogs is to brush often to remove shed hair.

- Shiba Inu
- Siberian Husky
- Spinone Italiano
- Sussex Spaniel
- Tibetan Spaniel
- Welsh Springer Spaniel

Tools

The core tools for grooming the medium coat are as follows:

- blow-dryer with low or cool setting
- coat rake
- hound glove

- pin brush
- rubber curry brush
- shedding comb

How to Do It

Every day, or at least once a week, give your dog a good brushing (as described in Chapter 4). During your monthly grooming sessions, after your dog has been bathed, follow this procedure:

1. Dry the medium coat with a towel. Air-drying the rest of the way is fine if you don't mind waiting a little longer for the coat to dry, especially in the case of thick double coats. Or finish with a blow-dryer.

2. To blow-dry, set the blow-dryer on low or cool and blow-dry the coat as you brush with a pin brush or natural bristle brush in the direction of hair growth. If the brush pulls out more dead coat, even better.

3. Once your dog is completely dry, have him stand. Step back and take a good look at his outline. Compare it to a picture of a well-groomed show dog of the same breed. How is the outline of the coat like or unlike the picture? Look for long, stray hairs too, as well as shaggy areas or other imbalances.

4. Using clippers, scissors, or a stripping knife (for plucking hairs, although you can do this with your fingers), neaten your dog's outline. Clip off hairs longer than the ones around them and straighten shaggy outlines that aren't supposed to be shaggy. Never clip

more than a few hairs without stopping and standing back to look again. If you trim at close range for too long, you can easily overdo the job. Remember, for medium coats, less is more!

5. Finally, and optionally, spray your dog's coat with a little coat conditioner to keep it resilient and easy to brush.

And that's all there is to grooming the medium coat. Aren't you glad you chose such an easy-care breed?

When blow-drying your dog, use the cool setting.

What Your Medium Coat Should Look Like

This photo gallery demonstrates what your well-groomed medium-coated dog should look like.

Akita

Coat: Outercoat is straight, harsh; undercoat is soft, dense.
Colors: Any color.
Grooming: Daily brushing.

Alaskan Malamute

Coat: Outercoat is thick, coarse; undercoat is dense, oily, woolly.
Colors: Solid white, mostly white with shadings from light gray to black, sable, red.
Grooming: Regular brushing.

American Eskimo Dog

Coat: Outercoat is long, straight; undercoat is thick, short; neck ruff.
Colors: Pure white, white with biscuit cream.
Grooming: Regular brushing and occasional going-over with a shedding blade.

Australian Cattle Dog

Coat: Outercoat is smooth, close, straight, hard, weather resistant; undercoat is short, dense.
Colors: Blue, red speckle.
Grooming: Regular brushing.

Australian Shepherd

Coat: Outercoat is medium texture and length, straight or wavy, weather resistant; undercoat varies with climate; moderate mane and frill.
Colors: Black, blue merle, red, red merle; may have white markings.
Grooming: Consistent care.

Belgian Malinois

Coat: Outercoat is short, straight, hard, dense, close fitting, weather resistant; undercoat is dense, woolly.
Colors: Rich fawn to mahogany; black mask; may have white markings.
Grooming: Easy-care coat; brush with bristle brush a few times a week.

Belgian Sheepdog

Coat: Outercoat is long, abundant, well fitting, straight guard hairs; undercoat is very dense, woolly; collarette around neck.
Colors: Black; may have white markings.
Grooming: Daily brushing.

Belgian Tervuren

Coat: Outercoat is long, abundant, well fitting, straight guard hairs; undercoat is dense, woolly; collarette around neck.
Colors: Rich fawn to russet mahogany, with black overlay; may have white markings.
Grooming: Coat requires regular attention to prevent matting.

Bernese Mountain Dog

Coat: Thick, soft, silky, fairly long; slightly wavy or straight.
Colors: Tricolor.
Grooming: Brush several times a week.

Border Collie

Coat: Rough variety has outercoat that is moderately long; undercoat is soft, short, dense. Smooth variety is shorter and coarser than rough variety.
Colors: All colors, combinations, markings.
Grooming: Regular brushing.

Borzoi

Coat: Long, silky coat can be flat, wavy, curly.
Colors: Any color or combination of colors.
Grooming: Generally brush every day or two.

Brittany

Coat: Dense, flat, or wavy; feathering.
Colors: Liver and white or orange and white with clear or roan patterns, tricolor; may have ticking.
Grooming: Weekly brushing.

Canaan Dog

Coat: Outercoat is straight, harsh, flat lying; undercoat is straight, soft, short, flat lying; slight ruff.
Colors: Predominantly white with mask, with or without patches of color; solid, with color ranging from black through all shades of brown.
Grooming: Regular brushing.

Cardigan Welsh Corgi

Coat: Outercoat is dense, slightly harsh, weather resistant; undercoat is short, soft, thick.
Colors: All shades of red, sable, brindle; black; blue merle; may have white markings.
Grooming: Regular brushing and combing required.

Cavalier King Charles Spaniel

Coat: Long, silky, straight, or slight wave; feathering.
Colors: Blenheim, tricolor, ruby, black and tan.
Grooming: Use a firm-bristled brush and wide-toothed comb several times a week.

Chesapeake Bay Retriever

Coat: Outercoat is water resistant, short, harsh, thick, oily; undercoat is woolly, dense, fine.
Colors: Any color of brown, sedge, deadgrass; white markings acceptable.
Grooming: Occasional brushing with a firm bristle brush.

Clumber Spaniel

Coat: Silky, dense, straight, flat, weather resistant; legs and chest well feathered.
Colors: Primarily white with lemon or orange markings.
Grooming: Regular brushing and combing. Abundant feathering and facial wrinkles require regular attention.

Collie (smooth)

Coat: Outercoat is short, hard, dense; undercoat is dense, soft, furry.
Colors: Sable and white, tricolor, blue merle and white; may have white, tan mrkings.
Grooming: Regular brushing.

English Springer Spaniel

Coat: Outercoat is medium length, straight, weather resistant; undercoat is short, soft, dense; can be wavy; moderate feathering.
Colors: Black and white, liver and white, tricolor, blue or liver roan.
Grooming: Regular brushing and attention to feathering.

Field Spaniel

Coat: Moderately long, flat or slightly wavy, silky, glossy, dense, water repellent; moderate feathering.
Colors: Black, liver, roan, golden liver; may have white or tan markings.
Grooming: Feathering requires special care.

Finnish Spitz

Coat: Outercoat is straight, long, harsh; undercoat is short, soft, dense.
Colors: Shades of reddish brown, golden red; may have white markings.
Grooming: Brush often when shedding. Otherwise easy-care coat.

Flat-Coated Retriever

Coat: Moderate length and density, straight or slightly wavy, glossy, flat lying, weather resistant; feathering.
Colors: Black, liver.
Grooming: Occasional brushing and combing.

German Shepherd Dog

Coat: Outercoat is medium length, straight, dense, harsh, close lying; undercoat is thick; may have neck ruff.
Colors: Most colors allowed except white.
Grooming: Regular brushing. Should not be bathed frequently or coat will lose natural oils.

Golden Retriever

Coat: Outercoat is straight or wavy, firm, dense, water repellent; good undercoat; neck ruff.
Colors: Various shades of golden.
Grooming: Brush several times a week.

Great Pyrenees

Coat: Outercoat is weather resistant, long, flat, thick, coarse; undercoat is dense, fine, woolly; neck ruff.
Colors: White, white with gray, badger, reddish brown; tan markings.
Grooming: Brush almost daily.

Kuvasz

Coat: Outercoat is quite wavy to straight, medium coarse; undercoat is fine, woolly; neck ruff.
Colors: White.
Grooming: Weekly brushing.

Norwegian Elkhound

Coat: Outercoat is longish, rough, dense, close lying.
Colors: Shining black.
Grooming: Regular brushing and combing.

Pembroke Welsh Corgi

Coat: Outercoat is longer, coarser than undercoat; undercoat is short, thick, weather resistant.
Colors: Red, sable, fawn, black and tan; may have white markings.
Grooming: Regular brushing and combing.

Saint Bernard

Coat: Shorthaired's outercoat is coarse, smooth, dense, close lying; undercoat is profuse. Longhaired's outercoat is medium length, plain to slightly wavy; undercoat is profuse. Neck ruff.
Colors: White with red of various shades, red of various shades with white, brindle and white; white markings.
Grooming: Brush once a week or so with a good, stiff brush.

Saluki

Coat: Feathered has smooth, soft, silky texture with slight feathering on legs and feathering at back of thighs. Smooth has same coat but without feathering.
Colors: White, cream, fawn, golden, red, grizzle and tan, tricolor, black and tan, or variations or these colors.
Grooming: Groom the feathered variety a few times a week with a bristle brush. Brush the smooth only occasionally.

Schipperke

Coat: Outercoat is straight, harsh, dense, abundant; undercoat is soft, thick. neck ruff.
Color: Black.
Grooming: Regular weekly brushing.

Shiba Inu

Coat: Outercoat is straight, stiff; undercoat is soft, thick.
Colors: Red, black and tan, sesame.
Grooming: Regular grooming with a stiff slicker brush at least once a week and more frequently during heavy shedding.

Siberian Husky

Coat: Outercoat is medium length, straight, soft, somewhat smooth lying; undercoat is soft, dense.
Colors: All colors from black to pure white; variety of markings may appear on head.
Grooming: Comb daily during shedding season. Otherwise easy-care coat.

Spinone Italiano

Coat: Flat or slightly crimped, slightly wiry, tough, dense; beard and mustache.
Colors: White, white with orange markings, white with peppered orange, white with brown markings, brown roan with or without brown markings.
Grooming: Weekly brushing.

Sussex Spaniel

Coat: Flat or slightly waved, abundant; feathering.
Color: Rich golden liver.
Grooming: Regular brushing and trimming.

Tibetan Spaniel

Coat: Outercoat is silky; undercoat is fine, dense.
Colors: All colors and combinations of colors acceptable.
Grooming: Occasional brushing and combing except during seasonal shed, when he requires daily attention.

Welsh Springer Spaniel

Coat: Straight, flat, soft, silky, waterproof, weatherproof; moderate feathering.
Colors: Rich red and white; any pattern is acceptable.
Grooming: Brushing and combing every few days.

9

GROOMING THE LONG COAT

Nothing quite compares to the glory of a perfectly groomed, long-coated dog trotting around the show ring, silky tresses flowing. It's no wonder the long-coated breeds so often win Best in Show! When it comes to grooming, the long coat is a true challenge but one that many pet owners relish.

I n this chapter, long-coated breeds are divided into three categories: those whose hair is parted down the middle and groomed accordingly; small long-coated dogs; and large long-coated dogs. Within each of these categories are different breeds, but grooming within each category is similar. Instructions are for all dogs within a category, with particular notes on individual breeds with a unique grooming requirement (such as the double topknot on the Maltese).

As with previous chapters, this is not a guide to high-end dog show grooming. This is a general guide for the pet owner who would like to keep the long-coated dog in his full coat. For more detailed show grooming instructions on your particular breed of long-coated dog, visit a professional groomer or breeder or contact your breed's national club for grooming information.

LONG HAIR, PARTED COAT

There are eight breeds with very long hair that should be parted along the back:

- Afghan Hound (puppy)
- Lhasa Apso
- Maltese
- Shih Tzu
- Silky Terrier
- Skye Terrier
- Tibetan Terrier
- Yorkshire Terrier

Although other breeds have long hair and some breeds (such as the Bearded Collie) may have hair that falls into a natural part, these eight breeds should be groomed with a very deliberate,

When it comes to grooming, the long coat is a true challenge but one that many pet owners relish.

perfectly straight part from the nape of the neck to the base of the tail.

Tools

You will need the following tools to groom your parted-coat breed:

- blow-dryer with cool setting
- comb (fine, medium, or wide, depending on coat thickness)
- electric clippers with a #10 blade (except for Afghan Hounds) plus a #15 blade for Yorkshire Terriers
- pin brush
- protein coat conditioner
- rubber bands, bows, ribbons, barrettes, etc., if you want to tie up your dog's topknot

- scissors, for shaping and trimming (when relevant)
- slicker brush (for daily mat removal in pets)

How to Do It

Parting these coats is arguably the most difficult part of grooming them, aside from a simple time investment to keep the coats mat-free. Here is your step-by-step, post-bath method for grooming your long, parted-coat breed.

1. After towel drying, blow-dry the long coat to keep it from drying into tangles. With the blow-dryer on cool or low, work from the bottom up, taking sections of hair with the pin brush and holding them out from the body. Keep the blow-dryer moving over each piece of hair until it is dry, then move up. Start with the legs and rear end and work your way up and forward. Keep brushing, fluffing, and straightening the coat so that it dries smoothly and free of tangles.

> The Shih Tzu is one of the longhaired breeds whose hair should be parted along the back.

2. When the coat is dry or almost dry, make the part. Stand behind your dog and put the tip of the comb just over the nose. Then slowly, 1 or 2

Doggy Colognes

It's not necessary to spray your pet with doggy cologne, but these sprays can be a nice way to keep him smelling good between baths.

inches (2.5 or 5 cm) at a time, move the comb over the crown of the head, down the nape, and down the back to the base of the tail. As you go, carefully move the hairs to the proper side.

3. If you finish and the part looks crooked, try again. Making a perfectly straight part isn't easy, but once you know how to do it, you'll feel like a pro. Be patient.

4. Once the coat is parted, spray it with coat conditioner or coat dressing to set the part. Now you can work on brushing the dog smooth on either side of the part.

5. Just as before the bath, brush thoroughly using the pin brush (or the slicker brush for heavily coated pets who still need some tangles removed), starting from the bottom and the back of the dog and working your way up and forward. Make sure that the hair lies smoothly and is tangle-free on either side of the part.

6. With a #10 blade on your electric clipper, shave your dog's anal area to keep it clean and free of long hair and tangles. Be careful not to touch the blade directly on your dog's skin. Or clip the area neatly with scissors.

7. With the same #10 blade, shave your dog's abdomen from groin to naval and down the insides of both thighs, except for Afghans, who should not be shaved.

8. Trim between your dog's paw pads with scissors, and trim around his feet so that the hair just reaches the ground evenly around the paw in a rounded shape.

9. If your dog's coat reaches the ground, scissor it neatly at floor level to keep it from interfering with his movement.

10. Brush out the hair on your dog's head, ears, and face.

11. If desired, tie up the topknot. (See next section.)

Breed-Specific Notes

The topknot is an attractive way to keep long hair out of your dog's eyes. The tied-up, ribbon-bedecked topknot is a traditional grooming practice for the Maltese, Shih Tzu, and Yorkshire Terrier and sometimes for the Afghan Hound and Lhasa Apso. The Skye Terrier, Tibetan Terrier, and Silky Terrier don't traditionally wear a topknot (Silky Terriers can usually see fine without one), but just

> Longhaired coats require more of a time investment than both smooth and medium coats do.

The topknot is an attractive way to keep long hair out of your dog's eyes.

Maltese

Most longhaired small breeds with a tied-up topknot wear a single tie in the center of the head. The Maltese, however, traditionally wears his topknot tied on either side of the part. To tie up the Maltese topknots, use the original middle part as a guide. Then part over each ear and make two topknots, one on either side of the part. Attach a latex rubber band and ribbon or barrette to each.

Yorkshire Terrier

With most small breeds, the ears are left natural, except for plucking of stray hairs inside the ears. Yorkshire Terriers, however, should have neater, cat-like ears kept free of fringe. Shave the tips of your Yorkie's ears with a #15 blade, inside and out, to 1/2 inch (1.5 cm), and scissor the hair to neaten.

LONG HAIR, SMALL BREEDS

Next, let's turn to the longhaired small breeds whose coats aren't parted along the back:

because your breed isn't formally groomed with a topknot doesn't mean that you can't tie one on anyway. Your longhaired pet may enjoy actually being able to *see* you!

To tie a topknot on your part-coated dog:

1. Part your dog's hair over each ear and in a line from ear to ear behind the ears. Draw the topknot together in your hands.
2. Secure with a latex rubber band. (You can buy these from a groomer or on the Internet.) Be careful not to attach the rubber band so that it pulls the hairs too tightly. A topknot should feel comfortable, not cause pain.
3. If desired, attach a bow or a barrette. You can buy an amazing array of hair accessories at pet stores and on the Internet. Or braid the topknot and attach a latex rubber band at the end of the braid.

> ## Beauty Tip
> Long coats easily become dry and brittle, and they should never be brushed when dry. For daily brushing as well as post-bath brushing, always spray long coats with a moisturizing coat conditioner and finish with a light spray of coat gloss containing oil. Regular moisturizing of long coats will keep them from breaking and splitting, resulting in a softer, fluffier, healthier, and more attractive coat.

The small breeds are easy to groom on a grooming table or even a bathroom counter. They tend to thrive on the attention and pampering of regular grooming sessions, and they love to spend that time with their people. Because many of these breeds spend a lot of time inside the house, they don't tend to get into underbrush or dirt as often (although a good romp in a muddy yard or dog park can result in an extended grooming session). However, these coats still need attention and plenty of it.

Some of the breeds listed need more frequent brushing and combing than others because some have longer and/or thicker hair than others. However, a daily grooming session is perfect for any small long-coated breed, whether it really needs it or not.

- Chihuahua (longhaired)
- Chinese Crested (powderpuff)
- Dachshund (Longhaired)
- English Toy Spaniel
- Havanese
- Japanese Chin
- Löwchen
- Papillon
- Pekingese
- Pomeranian

These frisky little longhaired fellows need lots of attention to their coats. Although none of these breeds have the sheer length of the parted-coat breeds, they all have long coats that can mat, tangle, and compromise both their beauty and good health.

Tools

You will need these tools to groom your long-coated small dog.

- blow-dryer with cool setting

Brush Up On a Breed

Afghan puppies should be groomed with a parted coat. However, once Afghans reach maturity, they grow in a smooth, shorthaired saddle along the back so that they no longer require parting. For this reason, the Afghan puppy is a parted-coat breed. The mature Afghan is actually a long-coated large breed and should be groomed accordingly. The biggest grooming challenge of the Afghan at any age? Time! It takes a long time to keep the tangles out of so much coat.

- comb (fine, medium, or wide, depending on coat thickness)
- electric clippers with a #10 blade
- pin brush
- protein coat conditioner
- scissors, for shaping and trimming (when relevant)
- slicker brush (for daily mat removal in pets)

How to Do It

The long-coated small breeds are characterized by a certain charming full fluffiness, as opposed to the parted-coat breeds, who are characterized by long, smooth, flowing hair, more akin to long human hair. For this reason, groom these dogs with fullness in mind: Think of the coat standing out from the body rather than lying flat against the skin.

After you've bathed your little dog, here is how to groom that long fluffy coat, step by step:

> The long-coated small breeds are characterized by a full fluffiness to the coat.

1. After towel-drying, blow-dry the long coat to keep it from drying into tangles. With the blow-dryer on cool or low, work from the bottom up, using the pin brush or slicker brush to fluff-dry. Take sections of hair with the pin brush or slicker brush and hold them out from the body as you blow-dry.

2. Keep the blow-dryer moving over each piece of hair until it is dry, then move up. Start with the legs and rear end and work your way up and forward. Keep brushing and fluffing for fullness, keeping the coat free from tangles.

3. Finish by running a metal comb through the coat to ensure that you haven't missed a single tangle or snag.

4. With a #10 blade on your electric clipper, shave your dog's anal area to keep it clean and free of long hair and tangles. Be careful not to touch the blade directly on your dog's skin. Or if you prefer, clip the area neatly with scissors.

5. Optionally, depending on your breed or if you like the ease of having your dog's underside free of long hair, with the same #10 blade, shave his abdomen from groin to naval and down the insides of both thighs. Shave *with* the lay of the hair.

6. Trim between your dog's paw pads with scissors, and if hair covers the feet, trim around the feet so that the hair just reaches the ground evenly around the paw in a rounded shape.

7. Brush and comb the hair on your dog's head, ears, and face.

8. Stand back and look at the dog's shape. Scissor any stray long hairs, but don't actually change the shape of the coat. Just look for uneven, stray areas that stand out after brushing.

9. To finish the dog and take the most advantage of fluffiness, spray the coat with coat conditioner or coat dressing to keep it soft and in place, then brush lightly over the top of the coat to set. Brush from the bottom up and from the shoulders forward to fluff the ruff. Fluff the tail, the body, the chest, the fringe—any area in which your longhaired small dog has a profuse coat.

10. Admire the beauty!

Breed-Specific Notes

A few of the breeds in this category have special grooming requirements.

Chinese Crested

The Chinese Crested comes in two varieties: hairless and powderpuff. To groom your hairless Chinese Crested, lightly brush the long tufts of hair on the head, ears, face, tail, and feet. To keep the hairless skin in good condition, moisturize your dog's skin by rubbing a few drops of baby oil between your palms and massaging it over his body. For the

Brush the Pomeranian against the lay of the hair to most dramatically enhance the coat's powderpuff effect.

powderpuff variety, groom according to the previous instructions to keep the long coat tangle-free and fluffy.

Havanese

The Havenese looks like a parted-coat breed, but his silky coat shouldn't be artificially parted. It may fall into a part, however, and this is natural. Some Havanese also have very wavy coats, which can naturally fall into cords. This is an acceptable coat type for the Havanese, making it look more like one of the curly-coated, corded breeds (which include the Puli and the Komondor).

Most of the long-coated small breeds without parted coats don't wear tied-up topknots, but because the Havanese has a long fall of hair, his topknot can be tied with an elastic band or braided or secured with barrettes on either side of the part. Although in his native Cuba the Havanese fall of hair protects this little breed's eyes from the sun and the topknot is never tied up, pet owners in this country often keep the hair out of their pets' eyes. However, according to the Havanese breed standard, groomers should never put bows or ribbons on the Havanese topknot. (If you would like to put one on your pet, though, we promise not to tell!)

Löwchen

The Löwchen is often clipped to look like a lion, with the hindquarters and base of the tail completely shaved, the head and ruff left full like a mane, and the tuft of the tail left full so that it can swish like a lion's tail. However, some people choose not to shave their little Löwchens in this way, preferring to leave the coat long or cut them down into a puppy cut for ease of care.

If you choose to groom your Löwchen according to the breed standard, use a 1/8-inch (.5-cm) comb on your electric clipper. Shave from the last rib back, leaving the full coat on the dog so that it covers the last rib. Shave the hindquarters all the way down to the hock or heel joint (in dogs the heel is the first joint up above the ground, not down by the paw), leaving a cuff of hair around the base of the foot. Clip the front legs from the elbow to the dewclaws (or to where they used to be if they are removed) so that the cuff of coat on the front legs matches the back legs in height. Clip the tail from the base to about halfway down the coat, leaving a tail plume. As for the rest of your Löwchen, the breed standard states that all unclipped areas should be left completely natural without any trimming, shaping, or scissoring. Do keep that Löwchen brushed and combed, however; otherwise, you'll have an unhappily matted little dog.

Pekingese and Pomeranian

Once they are dry, brush the Pekingese and the Pomeranian against the lay of the hair to most dramatically enhance the powderpuff effect of the coat.

LONG HAIR, LARGE BREEDS

The long-coated large breeds include the following:
- Afghan Hound (adult)
- Bearded Collie
- Briard
- Chow Chow
- Cocker Spaniel
- Collie (rough)
- English Cocker Spaniel
- English Setter
- Gordon Setter
- Irish Setter
- Keeshond
- Newfoundland
- Old English Sheepdog
- Samoyed

- Shetland Sheepdog

The longhaired large breeds are groomed similarly to the small breeds, but these larger long-coated dogs have some unique challenges of their own. The long-coated large breeds are more likely than their smaller counterparts to be working dogs, and spending time out in the field, the tundra, or the woods can result in a tangled, dirty, or debris-filled coat. Regular grooming and thorough brushing and combing are essential to keeping the working dog's long coat healthy.

Tools

You will need these tools to groom your long-coated large breed:
- blow-dryer with cool setting
- coat rake
- electric clippers with a #10 blade
- large pin brush
- large slicker brush (for daily mat removal in pets)
- natural bristle brush
- protein coat conditioner
- scissors, for shaping and trimming (when relevant)
- steel comb (medium or wide, depending on coat thickness)

The long-coated large breeds have profuse hair that needs special care. They take a long time to groom because their size means that they have so *much* of that thick, long coat.

Never brush a long-coated large dog without first spraying the coat with coat conditioner, or you could seriously compromise coat quality by breaking too much hair. Long coats dry out easily and can become brittle and fragile without conditioning. Before a bath, spray the dog well and brush out with a pin brush, working out tangled areas with the slicker brush and comb.

This category includes many different breeds with various types of coats, but in general, grooming instructions are the same. However,

Regular grooming and thorough brushing and combing are essential to keeping a longhaired working dog's coat healthy.

look for special instructions regarding the sporting breeds in this category at the end of this section.

How to Do It

After the bath, here is how to groom your long-coated large dog.

1. After towel-drying thoroughly, blow-dry the long coat to keep it from drying into tangles. With the blow-dryer on cool or low, work from the bottom up, using the pin brush or slicker brush.
2. When the coat is dry, work through it from the skin out with a metal comb to ensure that you haven't missed a single tangle or snag. If your dog is blowing his coat or shedding, pull out

excess coat with a coat rake. In heavily layered coats, work a layer at a time to be sure that you aren't leaving tangles and mats close to the skin.

3. Shave your dog's anal area to keep it clean and free of long hair and tangles. Be careful not to touch the blade directly on your dog's skin. Or clip the area neatly with scissors.
4. Trim between your dog's paw pads with scissors, and if hair covers the feet, trim around the feet so that the hair just reaches the ground evenly around the paw in a rounded shape.
5. Brush and comb the hair on your dog's head, ears, and face. Pluck hair out of the ears to neaten.
6. Stand back and look at the dog's shape. Scissor any stray long hairs, but don't actually change the shape of the coat. Just look for uneven stray areas that stand out after brushing.
7. To finish the dog and keep the coat in good shape, spray once more with coat conditioner, then brush lightly over the top of the coat to set. Fluff the tail (when relevant for your breed), the ruff, the chest, the fringe—any area in which your longhaired large dog has profuse coat.
8. Give your very patient long-coated dog a nice treat. It took a long time to groom that coat!

Breed-Specific Notes

Most of the long-coated large breeds must be carefully brushed and combed but have natural coats that should not be shaped or clipped. The sporting breeds are different. If you've chosen a long-coated sporting breed, grooming should include some very specific shaping with the electric clipper.

Cocker Spaniel

English Setter

Gordon Setter

Irish Setter

Sporting Breeds

Just follow these special instructions to groom your Cocker Spaniel, English Cocker Spaniel, English Setter, Gordon Setter, or Irish Setter after bathing and brushing. (See photographs on this page for individual clipping patterns.)

1. Clip the face along the jawbone and cheeks and the top and back of the head to keep the face clean.
2. Clip under the jaw and down the neck to about 1 or 2 inches (2.5 or 5 cm) above the breastbone, blending into the chest area.

3. Clip hair about a third of the way down each ear. Use a #10 blade on your electric clipper for large areas, a #15 for smaller areas.
4. Clip the body, including the tail, with a #7 blade, in the direction of hair growth. Leave the coat long along the legs and chest. Gradually blend the shorter back hair into the longer hair to avoid an obvious clipper line.
5. Proceed according to the remaining steps for all long-coated breeds, above.

What Your Long Coat Should Look Like

This photo gallery demonstrates what your well-groomed long-coated dog should look like.

Afghan Hound

Coat: Thick, silky, fine, with topknot of long hair.
Colors: All colors.
Grooming: Regular attention necessary. Coat must be washed before grooming to prevent coat damage.

Bearded Collie

Coat: Outercoat is flat, harsh, strong, shaggy; undercoat is soft, furry, close; beard.
Colors: Black, blue, brown, fawn; with or without white and tan markings.
Grooming: Regular weekly brushing.

Briard

Coat: Outercoat is long, coarse, shiny, hard, dry; undercoat is fine, tight; mustache and beard.
Colors: All uniform colors except white; may have white markings.
Grooming: Brush several times a week to prevent tangling.

Chihuhua (longhaired)

Coat: Soft, silky, flat, or slightly curly; neck ruff.
Colors: Any color.
Grooming: Brushing, bathing, and trimming necessary.

Chinese Crested (powderpuff)

Coat: Outercoat is straight, soft, silky; undercoat is short, silky.
Colors: Any color or combination of colors.
Grooming: Regular brushing, especially when shedding.

Chow Chow

Coat: Rough coat has outercoat that is abundant, dense, straight, offstanding, and coarse; undercoat is soft, thick, woolly. Smooth coat has outercoat that is hard, dense, smooth; definite undercoat.
Colors: Red, black, blue, fawn, cream.
Grooming: Both coat types require regular brushing with a steel comb. Facial wrinkles must be kept clean and dry.

Cocker Spaniel

Coat: Outercoat is medium length, silky, flat or slightly wavy; enough undercoat for protection; feathering.
Colors: Jet black, any solid color other than black, particolored.
Grooming: Demands regular attention; feathering needs special attention.

Collie (rough)

Coat: Outercoat is harsh, straight; undercoat is soft, furry, close.
Colors: Sable and white, tricolor, blue merle and white; may have white, tan markings.
Grooming: Regular brushing and combing.

Dachshund (Longhaired)

Coat: Outercoat is sleek, soft, glistening, straight or slightly wavy.
Colors: One-colored—red, cream/two-colored—black, chocolate, wild boar, gray, fawn, all with tan or cream markings/dappled.
Grooming: Brush regularly to prevent mats. The ears must be checked often.

English Cocker Spaniel

Coat: Double coat is medium length, flat or slightly wavy, silky; well feathered.
Colors: Various—solid colors are black, liver, red shades; particolors are clearly marked, ticked, or roaned and include black, liver, red shades, all with white; may have tan markings.
Grooming: Regular brushing—including feathering—required. Ears must be tended to almost daily.

English Setter

Coat: Long, flat, silky; feathering.
Colors: Black and white, orange and white, lemon and white, liver and white, tricolor.
Grooming: Regular brushing required. Ears must be checked regularly.

English Toy Spaniel

Coat: Profuse, long, straight or slightly wavy, silky, glossy; heavy fringing and feathering; mane.
Colors: Blenheim, Prince Charles, King Charles, Ruby.
Grooming: Frequent brushing required. Facial folds need frequent attention.

Gordon Setter

Coat: Straight or slightly wavy, soft, shiny.
Colors: Black with tan markings.
Grooming: Brush and comb coat every so often. Feathering must be kept free of tangles. Ears should be thoroughly cleaned.

Havanese

Coat: Outercoat is soft, abundant, flat, wavy or curly; undercoat is not well developed.
Colors: All colors.
Grooming: Long hair needs a lot of attention.

Irish Setter

Coat: Moderate length, straight, flat; feathering.
Colors: Rich chestnut red, mahogany; may have white markings.
Grooming: Brush and comb regularly, especially where there is profuse feathering.

Japanese Chin

Coat: Long, abundant, straight, silky; neck ruff.
Colors: Black and white, red and white, black and white with tan points.
Grooming: Brush and comb frequently.

Keeshond

Coat: Outercoat is long, straight, harsh; undercoat is thick, downy; neck ruff.
Colors: Mixture of gray, black, cream.
Grooming: Brush several times a week.

Lhasa Apso

Coat: Outercoat is long, straight, hard, heavy dense; undercoat is dense; whiskers and beard.
Colors: All colors and combinations.
Grooming: Brush the long coat daily to keep it dirt- and mat-free; can be kept in a clipped coat for ease of care.

Löwchen

Coat: Coat: Long, moderately soft, wavy, dense.
Colors: All colors and combinations.
Grooming: Brush regularly. A shorter clip may be employed for ease of care.

Maltese

Coat: Long, flat, silky, dense.
Colors: Pure white; light tan or lemon markings permissible.
Grooming: The long coat must be brushed and combed frequently. A shorter clip may be employed for ease of care.

Newfoundland

Coat: Outercoat is moderately long, moderately straight, coarse, oily, water resistant; undercoat is soft, dense.
Colors: Black, brown, gray, white with black markings.
Grooming: Brush frequently. Ears should be checked often to prevent infection.

Old English Sheepdog

Coat: Outercoat is not straight, harsh, profuse; undercoat is waterproof pile.
Colors: Any shade of gray, grizzle, blue, blue merle with or without white markings or in reverse.
Grooming: Thick undercoat must be brushed and combed often to keep it from matting. Non-show dogs can have coat clipped to make it more manageable.

Papillon

Coat: Long, straight, fine, silky, flowing, abundant; chest frill; feathering.
Colors: Particolor.
Grooming: Brush regularly to prevent matting, but his coat is quite easy to care for.

Pekingese

Coat: Outercoat is long, straight, coarse, standoff; undercoat is thick, soft; mane; some feathering.
Colors: All colors and markings; may have black mask.
Grooming: Daily attention—brushing and combing—required.

Pomeranian

Coat: Outercoat is long, straight, harsh, glistening; undercoat is soft, fluffy, thick; neck ruff.
Colors: All colors, patterns, variations.
Grooming: Regular attention required—brush several times a week.

Samoyed

Coat: Outercoat is harsh, standoff, weather resistant; undercoat is shorter, soft, thick, close, woolly; neck ruff.
Colors: Pure white, white and biscuit, cream, all biscuit.
Grooming: Brush or comb two to three times a week. Daily brushing or combing required during heavy sheds (once or twice a year).

Shetland Sheepdog

Coat: Outercoat is long, straight, harsh; undercoat is short, furry, dense; mane.
Colors: Black, blue merle, shades of sable, all marked with varying amounts of white and/or tan.
Grooming: Brush every few days.

Shih Tzu

Coat: Outercoat is long, flowing, luxurious, dense; undercoat is "good."
Colors: All colors permissible.
Grooming: The long coat should be brushed daily to prevent tangles and mats, and a topknot should be maintained. A shorter clip may be employed for ease of care.

Silky Terrier

Coat: Flat, fine, glossy, silky.
Colors: Blue and tan.
Grooming: The long coat must be brushed or combed out every day and bathed regularly. A topknot may be maintained. A shorter clip may be employed for ease of care.

Skye Terrier

Coat: Outercoat is long, straight, flat, hard; undercoat is short, soft, woolly, close lying; feathering.
Colors: Black, blue, dark or light gray, silver platinum, fawn, cream.
Grooming: Brush once a week to prevent mats.

Tibetan Terrier

Coat: Outercoat is long, wavy or straight, fine, profuse; undercoat is soft, woolly.
Colors: Any color or combination of colors.
Grooming: Brush and comb frequently. A shorter clip may be employed for ease of care.

Yorkshire Terrier

Coat: Moderately long, straight, silky, glossy, fine.
Colors: Steel blue and tan.
Grooming: The long coat must be brushed and combed every day. A topknot will keep long hair out of the eyes. A shorter clip may be employed for ease of care.

10

GROOMING THE WIRE COAT

The wire coat is unique in texture and appearance: It gives that scruffy, whiskery character to the breeds that have it. The proper wire coat shouldn't be soft, fuzzy, or silky. It should be hard and crisp, like beard hair. It should also be groomed in a manner different than any other coat type to maintain its crisp texture and to keep it bright in color and free of dead hairs. This involves "stripping" and "plucking" the hair to achieve the desired look. Some pet owners choose to shave down their wirehaired pets rather than endure the task of properly grooming the wire coat. This is certainly an option for pet owners who don't mind a softer coat, but shaving it will cause it to grow back softer and duller in color.

Although plucking or stripping wire coats is essentially the same for all breeds, different breeds within the wire coat category have different shapes, and ultimately, different grooming procedures required in addition to plucking or stripping.

The breeds in this chapter are all groomed similarly (although not identically) to the Miniature Schnauzer. Some breed fans will be horrified if you groom a long-legged wire breed to look exactly like a Schnauzer, but for many, this clip is practical and easy to maintain. For exact grooming instructions for your breed, consult your national or local breed club or a professional show groomer.

TOOLS

These tools are required to groom the wire coat.
- blow-dryer with cool setting
- combination medium/fine-toothed comb
- electric clippers with a variety of blade sizes as relevant for breed, for shaping and keeping anal area clean
- hound glove or terrier mitt
- natural bristle brush
- scissors, for shaping and trimming
- shedding comb
- slicker brush
- stripping knife

For purists who want their wirehaired dogs to look properly wiry and whiskery, the procedure for grooming the wire coat is to strip or pluck it.

WIREHAIRED GROOMING TERMINOLOGY AND TECHNIQUES

Wirehaired coats have special grooming terminology and techniques all their own. The wirehaired coat doesn't really shed, which is why wirehaired breeds are sometimes good for allergy sufferers. Instead, the hairs grow longer and become looser in the

The proper wire coat should be hard and crisp, like beard hair.

The procedure for grooming the wire coat is to strip or pluck it.

coat but look unruly and dull in color. The proper way to groom a wirehaired coat is to pluck it or strip it or do both. Plucking or stripping are methods of removing the hairs by pulling them out with the fingers (plucking) or with a special tool called a stripping knife (stripping). A stripping knife isn't sharp. It simply provides a flat metal surface to grip the hair between the blade and your thumb.

Plucking or stripping the longer, older, duller hairs keeps the skin healthy and stimulated and makes room for newer, brighter hairs to grow in. It keeps the dog looking neat and well groomed, and it's even kind of fun. However, it takes a long time, especially on a large dog.

Your groomer may not do the procedure for you, either, and even if she did, you would probably have to pay dearly because it is so time consuming. Most wirehaired pet owners are better off learning the technique themselves (or again, shaving down their pets periodically).

Stages and Schedules

Wirehaired coats grow in three stages: new growth, old growth, and in-between growth. Keeping these stages in mind, plucking and stripping can be done on one of two schedules: rolling the coat or taking the coat down.

Rolling the coat means plucking or stripping little bits at a time—a few plucks of hair here and there every day all year round. Rolling the coat leaves some of all three stages of hair in the coat at all times but diligently removes old coat on a regular basis to keep new growth coming in and to keep color bright.

The other option, and one more commonly practiced by show dog handlers and breeders, is to take the coat all the way down. That means doing a massive plucking or stripping job all at one time to completely remove the old growth in one fell swoop and allow lots of brand-new bright coat to grow in all at once. With the Schnauzer, this is done in stages over a four-week period. Body coat is done the first week, followed by hindquarters, neck, and head. In this manner, the hair grows to the appropriate lengths for the show ring. The undercoat should be stripped after all the hard wire coat is removed.

Taking the coat all the way down two to three months before an important dog show can result in a beautiful wiry coat, but for most pet owners who may not even be able to tell the difference, rolling the coat is much easier to practice. Most of us can spare a few minutes each day more easily than an entire afternoon taking down a coat.

For the purposes of this book, we will assume that you choose to roll

With the Schnauzer, stripping is done in stages over a four-week period to achieve the desired coat.

the coat or pluck or strip out small amounts on a regular basis.

Plucking

Plucking the coat is probably the easiest method because you don't have to learn to manipulate the stripping knife, and your only tools are your own two hands—and possibly some grooming powder. Many show dog groomers agree that plucking (sometimes called "hand-stripping") is also the superior method, as it targets individual hairs more precisely and can result in a more thorough job. It takes longer than stripping, however, because you will take out fewer hairs with each pull.

However, if you pull the hair carelessly, straight up, or not in the direction of hair growth, or if you pull without holding the skin taut with your opposite hand, you could irritate your dog, so practice, practice, practice, and always take just a

few hairs at a time to keep the procedure pleasant. (And don't forget periodic treats to reward your dog for being so patient.) Done correctly, plucking should not be painful or uncomfortable for your dog. Dog skin is less sensitive and much looser than human skin.

Now let's get to the plucking procedure. To practice, begin on the back toward your dog's hind end, as this area is easily accessible. To pluck, first hold the skin taut above where you will pluck with your nondominant hand. If desired, sprinkle a little grooming powder over the area to make the hairs easier to grip. With your dominant hand, grasp just a few hairs (really, just a few) and pull them down and straight out in the direction of hair growth.

Keeping the skin taut will help keep this procedure painless for your dog, and you'll be better able to see which hairs to pluck. The new growth should stay firmly rooted and the longer, old growth should come out more easily. Once you get the hang of it, you can pluck in a regular fashion, doing a certain area each week or working your way in a certain pattern to cover all parts of your dog. Here is one suggested method:

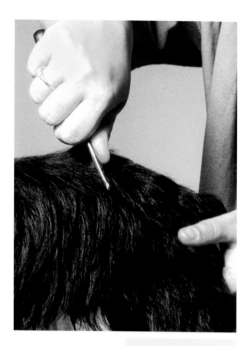

Stripping with a stripping knife is faster than plucking but may be less precise.

Ask the Groomer

Q: What is a terrier mitt?

A: The terrier mitt is a special kind of grooming brush that slips over the hand. Designed to stimulate the skin, loosen dead coat, and keep new coat tight and dense, the terrier mitt is perfect for all wirehaired breeds. Although it isn't an absolutely necessary tool, you may find that it becomes your favorite grooming item for your wirehaired dog.

1. Begin by plucking from the withers (shoulders) to the base of the tail.
2. Then pluck from the neck to tail on each side, to cover the entire torso.
3. Scissor around the anal area to keep it free of stray hairs.
4. Remove hair down each leg, then from chest to belly to avoid a skirted appearance (especially in short-legged terriers like Scotties and Westies).
5. Pluck the neck, throat, and head.
6. Remove all long stray hairs from the face and around the eyes.
7. Pluck all long hairs from inside and outside the ears.

Heads Up

Wirehaired terriers should have any of three different head shapes when grooming is complete: rectangular, cylindrical, or round.

Rectangular heads contain long, square, angular beards and protruding eyebrows. The terriers with rectangular heads include the Airedale, Lakeland, Scottish, and Sealyham Terriers and the Miniature Schnauzer. The distinctive eyebrows should be trimmed. Start by combing the eyebrow forward, then place the flat side of the scissors beside the outer corner of the eye. Point the blade tip toward the center of the nose and make a straight, smooth cut. The Border Terrier has a wide head, but his eyebrows should be removed, and the breed has a natural mustache but no beard.

Cylindrical heads have shorter beards, protruding eyebrows, and a more rounded shape to the crown and muzzle. These include the Irish, Parson and Jack Russell, Welsh, and Wire Fox Terriers. These heads are trimmed to be narrower, and the beards should be somewhat shorter than the typical Schnauzer beard.

Finally, a handful of terriers have rounded heads with full face furnishings, no beards, and no defined eyebrows. Instead, they have full faces with mane-like furnishings. These include the Australian, Cairn, Dandie Dinmont, Norfolk, Norwich, and West Highland White Terriers.

Stripping

Stripping with a stripping knife is faster than plucking but may be less precise. When you are pressed for time, however, the stripping knife can be your best friend. The stripping knife looks like a straight comb but with shallow teeth. It should be very dull so that it doesn't cut off the hairs but instead helps you pull them from the root.

To strip your dog:

1. Hold the comb in your dominant hand and catch up a small amount of hair in the comb with your thumb.
2. Pull it out firmly in the direction of coat growth. Don't twist your wrist or pull up, or the hair could break off. Pull it out straight from the root.
3. Work over the coat in the same order as listed above for plucking.

THE LONG-LEGGED TERRIERS

The long-legged wirehaired terriers include the following:

- Airedale Terrier
- Border Terrier
- Giant Schnauzer
- Irish Terrier
- Lakeland Terrier
- Miniature Schnauzer
- Parson and Jack Russell Terriers (wirehaired)
- Soft Coated Wheaten Terrier
- Standard Schnauzer
- Welsh Terrier
- Wire Fox Terrier

How to Do It

Here are basic instructions on how to groom your long-legged wirehaired dog:

1. Begin with a good, thorough brushing with a natural bristle brush, a slicker brush, and a shedding comb or fine-toothed comb to remove as much loose coat as possible, to

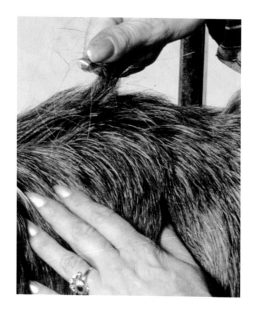

5. Trim the chest hair and underbelly hair with scissors to neaten and shape as necessary.

6. Shave the abdomen/groin area.

7. Shave or clip carefully around the anal area and under the tail.

8. Remember to maintain a smooth line from clipped to unclipped portions of the body.

9. Clip or pluck hair from inside and outside the ears, and shave or trim to neaten.

10. Clip the head to neaten and shape. Comb and shape the eyebrows, beard, and/or mustache hair (as relevant) forward and neaten to attain the proper head shape for your breed. (See sidebar "Heads Up.")

11. If you decide to pluck or strip, do so according to the instructions above. A major plucking or stripping a couple of times a year when the coat begins to look particularly long and dull (a sign that the coat is "blown") will keep it in show condition.

THE SHORT-LEGGED TERRIERS

The short-legged wirehaired terriers include the following:

- Australian Terrier
- Cairn Terrier
- Dandie Dinmont Terrier

stimulate the skin, and to loosen dead coat to make plucking easier.

> **Your stripping knife should be very dull so that it doesn't cut off the hairs but instead helps you pull them from the root.**

2. After bathing, blow-dry while brushing until the coat is dry.

3. Decide if you want to maintain a stripped dog or if you want to take the easy route and clip your dog. As mentioned earlier, many pet owners clip their wirehaired dogs because this is a quick and easy way to maintain their pets.

4. If you decide to clip, use a #7, #8, or #10 blade to clip the body coat to approximately 1/4 inch (.5 cm) in length. Clip from the neck to tail base, clip body sides, and for Schnauzers only, clip halfway down the rear legs along the back. Leave the front legs, belly, and the inside of the back legs unclipped.

The Scottish Terrier is an example of a short-legged terrier.

- Norfolk Terrier
- Norwich Terrier
- Scottish Terrier
- Sealyham Terrier
- West Highland White Terrier

The short-legged terriers are all groomed similarly (although not identically) to the Scottish Terrier, with the exception of differing head shapes; most of the short-legged wirehaired terriers have round heads, with the exception of the Scottish Terrier and the Sealyham Terrier, with their dramatically rectangular heads.

For exact grooming instructions for your breed, consult your national or local breed club or professional show groomer.

Most short-legged terriers have round heads.

How to Do It

Here are basic instructions on how to groom your short-legged wirehaired terrier.

1. Begin with a good, thorough brushing with a natural bristle brush, a slicker brush, and a shedding comb or fine-toothed comb to remove as much loose coat as possible, to stimulate the skin, and to loosen dead coat to make plucking easier.

2. After bathing, blow-dry while brushing until the coat is dry.

3. Decide if you want to maintain a stripped dog or if you want to take the easy route and clip

your dog. As mentioned earlier, many pet owners clip their wirehaired dogs because this is a quick and easy way to maintain their pets.

4. If you decide to clip, use a #5, #7, or #8 blade to clip the body coat to approximately 1/4 inch (.5 cm) in length.

5. Clip from the neck to the tail base and about halfway down the tail, blending clipped hair into unclipped.

6. Clip body sides to about the level of the first leg joint so that the clipped area extends in a straight line from front to back, parallel to the floor. To avoid a hula skirt look, blend the clipped area into the unclipped area.

7. Clip the chest from under the muzzle to about 1 inch (2.5 cm) above the breastbone.

8. Leave the front legs, belly, and the inside of the back legs unclipped.

9. Trim chest and underbelly hair with scissors to neaten and shape as necessary.

10. Shave the abdomen/groin area.

11. Shave or clip carefully around the anal area and under the tail.

12. Remember to maintain a smooth line from clipped to unclipped portions of the body.

The wirehaired hound breeds are distinguished by their natural look.

13. Clip or pluck hair from inside and outside the ears and shave or trim to neaten.

14. Clip the head to neaten and shape. Comb and shape the eyebrows, beard, and/or mustache hair (as relevant) forward and neaten to attain the proper head shape for your breed. (See sidebar "Heads Up.")

15. If you decide to pluck or strip, do so according to the instructions above. A major plucking or stripping a couple of times a year when the coat begins to look particularly long and dull (a sign that the coat is "blown") will keep it in show condition.

Beauty Tip

If you choose to roll the coat, you won't achieve a full show coat for almost half a year because the gradual removal of old coat results in a gradual replacement with new coat at a much slower rate. Taking the coat all the way down will bring in a bright new show coat in a much shorter time (about two to three months), but it is a lot more work and not necessary for the pet owner.

OTHER WIREHAIRED DOGS

The German Wirehaired Pointer is an example of a sporting wirehaired breed.

Not every wirehaired dog is a terrier, even though these are the breeds people most often picture with wiry coats. Wirehaired breeds appear in every group except Non-Sporting, and while every wirehaired breed *can* be stripped or plucked, each breed within the following groups has individual grooming requirements. Let's go over them group by group.

Herding

The Bouvier des Flandres is the notable wirehaired herding breed. Similar in look to a Giant Schnauzer, the Bouvier should be groomed in a like manner. Dry the thick, heavy coat, comb with a steel comb, shave the ears with a #10 blade from base to tip, and hand-strip the face, leaving tall, erect eyebrows and a wide, thick beard. This is time consuming because the Bouvier is such a large dog. The head should not be clipped.

Scissor around the anal area and feet to neaten but leave the rest of the coat natural, as it is designed to protect against harsh weather conditions and is characteristic of the breed. If you really would rather keep your Bouvier in a shorter coat, you can clip the body down with a #7 or #5 blade in the way you would clip a Schnauzer. The Bouvier is prone to sunburn if clipped too short, so be careful.

Hound

The wirehaired hound breeds are distinguished by their natural look. As a rule, these breeds shouldn't be trimmed or shaped in any way, but they should be brushed and combed thoroughly and periodically plucked or stripped to keep the coat clean and bright. This group includes the following: the Dachshund (Wirehaired), Irish Wolfhound, Otterhound, Petit Basset Griffon Vendéen (PBGV), and the Scottish Deerhound.

The Wirehaired Dachshund may require some neatening of his beard and the underbelly hair may need a bit of trimming, but other than that, roll

these coats or brush and comb them thoroughly and you will find that they are pretty easy to care for. Keep the Otterhound and the PBGV brushed often to prevent mats because these coats are longer and dense. The biggest challenge with the Irish Wolfhound and the Scottish Deerhound is their sheer size.

Sporting

This group includes the gundogs with wire coats: the German Wirehaired Pointer and the Wirehaired Pointing Griffon.

For the German Wirehaired Pointer, after bathing and drying, pluck the coat with your fingers or a stripping knife. Keep the face clipped to about 1.5 inches (4 cm) but leave the beard and eyebrows. Pluck longer hairs from the body and legs. Or clip the body and

The Bouvier des Flandres is the notable wirehaired herding breed.

head with a #7 blade on an electric clipper, but leave hair on the rib cage and underside of the legs and leave the beard and eyebrows.

For the Wirehaired Pointing Griffon, leave the coat in its natural, unkempt, medium length. Pluck or clip only on the ears, top of the head, cheeks, and feet. Leave the rest of the coat in its natural state, but brush frequently to remove dead coat. This breed should have a prominent mustache and eyebrows but not a beard.

Brush Up on a Breed

Have you noticed that a large number of the wire-coated breeds come from the British Isles? The weather-resistant wire coat is particularly helpful for enduring the harsh, wet climate of the British Isles and for doing the work required of so many of the British breeds: outdoor farm work such as herding sheep and controlling vermin.

Toy

The two wirehaired toy breeds are the Affenpinscher and Brussels Griffon.

These little fellows are small, so they are relatively easy to hand-strip, and they should be kept in a natural coat unshaped by an electric clipper. Trim extra hair between the foot pads, neaten the ears, and pluck a few areas evenly around the coat every day and your little toy dog will look as feisty as any terrier.

The Affenpinscher is a wirehaired toy breed.

Working

The Giant and Standard Schnauzers are officially working breeds, but they should be groomed exactly like the Miniature Schnauzer, as described earlier in the long-legged terrier section.

What Your Wirehaired Coat Should Look Like

This photo gallery demonstrates what your well-groomed wirehaired dog should look like.

Affenpinscher

Coat: Dense, rough, harsh; longer hair on head, eyebrows, beard.
Colors: Black, black and tan, gray, silver; may have mask.
Grooming: Regular brushing several times a week; trimming required.

Airedale Terrier

Coat: Outercoat is wiry, hard, dense; undercoat is soft, downy; coat lies straight and close.
Colors: Body saddle is tan with black or dark grizzle on sides and upper body.
Grooming: Strip if being shown; clip if not. Brush daily.

Australian Terrier

Coat: Outercoat is harsh, straight, dense; undercoat is short, soft; topknot; neck ruff.
Colors: Solid red, solid sandy, various shades of blue and tan; light-colored topknot.
Grooming: Regular brushing and trimming.

Border Terrier

Coat: Outercoat is very wiry, somewhat broken, close lying; undercoat is short, dense.
Colors: Blue and tan, grizzle and tan, red, wheaten; may have white markings.
Grooming: Coat can be left in its natural state. Brush occasionally with a slicker brush. Does not need to be stripped unless being shown.

Bouvier des Flandres

Coat: Outercoat is rough, harsh, dry; undercoat is fine, soft, dense, waterproof; thick mustache and beard.
Colors: Shades of fawn to black; may have white marking.
Grooming: Brush several times a week; hair should be trimmed several times a year.

Brussels Griffon

Coat: Wiry, hard, dense; beard and mustache.
Colors: Black, red, black and tan, beige.
Grooming: Professional grooming required; must be hand-stripped.

Cairn Terrier

Coat: Outercoat is harsh, profuse; undercoat is short, soft, close, furry.
Colors: Any color except white.
Grooming: Regular brushing, with trimming around the eyes. Professional grooming several times a year to keep coat plucked is advised.

Dandie Dinmont Terrier

Coat: Outercoat is crisp, hard; undercoat is soft, linty.
Colors: Pepper, mustard.
Grooming: For show, professional grooming required.

German Wirehaired Pointer

Coat: Outercoat is harsh, dense, flat lying; undercoat is dense; beard.
Colors: Solid liver, liver and white.
Grooming: Brush weekly with a stiff bristle brush. Outercoat may need to be stripped.

Giant Schnauzer

Coat: Outercoat is wiry, harsh, dense, strong; undercoat is soft; beard.
Colors: Solid black, salt and pepper; dark mask in salt and pepper coloration.
Grooming: Regular brushing and trimming required. Clip several times a year to maintain coat. Beard, eyebrows, and ears must be trimmed.

Irish Terrier

Coat: Outercoat is wiry, stiff, dense; undercoat is softer; may have slight beard.
Colors: Whole-colored bright red, golden red, red wheaten, wheaten.
Grooming: Hand-plucking advised. Regular brushing and combing required.

Irish Wolfhound

Coat: Rough and hard on body; beard and hair over eyes long and wiry.
Colors: Gray, brindle, red, black, pure white, fawn, or any other color that appears in the Deerhound.
Grooming: Regular brushing and combing required. Professional plucking advised.

Lakeland Terrier

Coat: Outercoat is wiry, hard, weather resistant; undercoat is soft, close lying.
Colors: Blue, black, liver, red, wheaten, black and tan, blue and tan, red grizzle.
Grooming: Regular hand-plucking required.

Miniature Schnauzer

Coat: Outercoat is hard, wiry; undercoat is soft, close, dense.
Colors: Salt and pepper, black and silver, solid black.
Grooming: Stripping or clipping required.

Norfolk Terrier

Coat: Outercoat is straight, wiry, hard, close lying; definite undercoat.
Colors: All shades of red, wheaten, black and tan, grizzle.
Grooming: Almost daily brushing and combing required. Ask a professional groomer about clipping.

Norwich Terrier

Coat: Outercoat is straight, wiry, hard, close lying; definite undercoat.
Colors: All shades of red, wheaten, black and tan, grizzle.
Grooming: Almost daily brushing and combing required. Ask a professional groomer about clipping.

Otterhound

Coat: Outercoat is long, rough, harsh, dense, waterproof; evident undercoat.
Colors: Any color or color combination.
Grooming: Brush several times a week.

Petit Basset Griffon Vendéen

Coat: Outercoat is long, rough; undercoat is thick; beard and mustache.
Colors: White with any combination of lemon, orange, tricolor, grizzle markings; also black, sable markings.
Grooming: Brushing and combing required.

Scottish Deerhound

Coat: Harsh, shaggy, thick, close lying; beard and mustache.
Colors: Dark blue-gray, darker and lighter gray shades, brindles and yellows, sandy red or red fawn with black points.
Grooming: Go over with a comb or brush once or twice a week.

Scottish Terrier

Coat: Outercoat is intensely hard, wiry, close lying; undercoat is short, dense, soft.
Colors: Black, wheaten, brindle of any color.
Grooming: Brush or comb a few times a week. Stripping his "jacket" every several months preserves the outercoat's harsh texture.

Sealyham Terrier

Coat: Outercoat is long, hard, wiry; undercoat is soft, dense, weather resistant.
Colors: All white or with lemon, brown, or badger pied markings on head and ears.
Grooming: Comb or brush at least twice weekly. Clip or strip every two to three months.

Soft Coated Wheaten Terrier

Coat: Soft, silky, gently waved or curled, abundant.
Colors: Any shade of wheaten.
Grooming: Brush or comb every day or two. Bathe at least every other month. Trim straggly hairs regularly.

Standard Schnauzer

Coat: Outercoat is hard, wiry, tight, very thick; undercoat is soft, close, dense; beard.
Colors: Pepper and salt, pure black.
Grooming: Daily brushing of longer furnishings. For showing, stripping may be necessary; a pet Schnauzer can be clipped instead.

West Highland White Terrier

Coat: Outercoat is straight, harsh; undercoat is short, soft, close.
Color: White.
Grooming: Simple brushing and combing. Hand-strip several times a year.

Wire Fox Terrier

Coat: Outercoat is very wiry, hard, dense; undercoat is soft, dense.
Colors: Predominantly white with black, black and tan, or tan markings.
Grooming: Professional grooming required for hand-stripping. If done several times a year, he will need only occasional brushing.

Wirehaired Pointing Griffon

Coat: Outercoat is medium length, straight, harsh, coarse; undercoat is fine, thick, downy; mustache.
Colors: Steel gray with liver brown patches, liver roan, liver, liver and white, orange and white.
Grooming: Occasional brushing necessary. Should see a professional groomer for twice-yearly stripping.

11

GROOMING THE CURLY OR WAVY COAT

Finally, we come to the curly coat—the most famous of grooming challenges and the coat worn by that most famously groomed of breeds, the Poodle. Curly or wavy coats aren't always difficult to maintain, depending on what you decide to do with them. Keeping a standard Poodle in constant full show regalia is practically a full-time job, while your marcelled American Water Spaniel or corded Puli won't require nearly the time investment. Yet even these breeds take time and care to maintain a show-quality coat.

S ome of the wavy- and curly-coated breeds have single coats that continue to grow like human hair, and some have double coats with woolly undercoats. While the undercoated curls tend to mat more quickly, all curly and wavy coats, by their very nature, are prone to mat because the hairs curl back on themselves and knot easily.

For this reason, these coats must be brushed and combed—and often! The exception is the corded coat, which should be teased out with the fingers to encourage the natural, mat-free cord formation. Also, for breeds with crisp curls like the Irish Water Spaniel, wash and shape without brushing during the drying process to keep the curls intact. Curly coats tangle and knot easily. They also tend to be dry and should always be sprayed with a coat dressing, oil spray, or some water with conditioner or cream rinse mixed in before brushing; brushing a dry coat will result in breakage.

Because of the challenging nature of the curly/wavy coat, many pet owners decide to keep their pets clipped down in an easy-care pet clip. Even so, many of the curly-coated breeds (particularly the Bichon Frise, the Poodle, and the terriers) require a certain amount of shaping and trimming to match the breed standard so that they will have the look of their breed. A monthly trip to the groomer or even a monthly wielding of the clippers at home will keep curly coats under control. When in doubt, pets can always be cut down without compromising the curly coat. The key is to keep these breeds brushed, combed, and tangle-free.

For most pet owners, keeping the coat trimmed to a manageable length of a couple inches

Breeds with a corded coat, like the Puli, should be teased out with the fingers to encourage the natural, mat-free cord formation.

(cm) is by far the most practical solution. Even in relatively easy-care coats, however, the wavy and curly-coated breeds still require lots of grooming, and even at a short length, should not usually be brushed without a protective spray of conditioner or oil applied first.

TOOLS

To groom your wavy- or curly-coated dog, have the following tools ready:

- coat dressing or coat oil spray
- combination medium/fine-toothed metal comb
- electric clippers with a variety of blade sizes as relevant for breed, for shaping and keeping anal area clean
- natural bristle brush
- pin brush
- scissors, for shaping and trimming

- shedding comb
- slicer brush

The wavy/curly-coated breeds fall naturally into several categories: the sporting/water breeds, the herding breeds, the terriers, and the non-sporting (and toy, with regard to the Toy Poodle) breeds. Let's look in more detail at how to groom your dog by beginning with a look at this unique coat type.

THE WATER BREEDS

The water breeds include the following:

- American Water Spaniel
- Curly-Coated Retriever
- Irish Water Spaniel
- Portuguese Water Dog

These breeds are sporting dogs with harsh curly coats. Because they typically spend a lot of time out in the field, retrieving from water, flushing upland game, and serving as all-purpose hunting companions, their coats should be kept short and neat. Long straggly curls will latch onto every stray twig, bur, and piece of underbrush with which they come into contact.

Show coats are scissored into a neat shape, and this precise scissoring of the curly coat is labor intensive. Those who keep curly-coated sporting breeds for hunting and as pets are much more likely to clip them down with

Curly coats must be brush and combed often.

an electric clipper to a length of about 2 inches (5 cm) (with the exception of the Curly-Coated Retriever, whose coat is short enough that it doesn't require clipping).

The American Water Spaniel's close, curly, or marcelled coat can be kept trimmed short or scissored to shape.

Here is how to groom your wavy- or curly-coated sporting breed.

1. Before bathing, brush out the entire coat with a pin brush and/or slicker brush to remove as much dead coat as possible and to detangle. Tackle mats with a mat comb or coat rake, or cut through them with a scissors to remove. (See Chapter 15 for more on how to remove a mat.)
2. Run a comb through the entire coat to be sure that you removed every tangle.
3. Scissor the leg hair evenly, removing excess hair.
4. Cut hair from under the foot and between the foot pads. The foot should appear rounded and should blend in with the leg hair, appearing like a powderpuff over the foot.
5. Clip down the torso to 2 inches (5 cm), or scissor off fuzz and shape by scissoring the sides to neaten. Shape the sides and rear to best match the shape of the breed. An imperfect form can be slightly adjusted by the shape in which you trim the curly coat. Take off just a little at a time, periodically standing back to examine the shape of the dog and to compare it to a picture of a well-groomed specimen of your breed.
6. After the bath, do not blow-dry or brush the body coat. Let the curls, waves, or marcels (continuous waves) air-dry naturally so that they stay intact.

In addition, each of the individual sporting breeds with curly or wavy coats requires certain individual adjustments, even for pets.

American Water Spaniel

The American Water Spaniel's close, curly, or marcelled coat can be kept trimmed short or scissored to shape. This breed has more feathering on the tail and legs than the Irish Water Spaniel but is otherwise groomed in a similar fashion. Trim feathers on the underside of the tail to neaten into a sickle shape and to remove stray long hairs, but in general, leave the outline of this breed so that it is natural. Be sure to keep those flowing ears tangle-free!

Curly-Coated Retriever

The Curly-Coated Retriever has a short coat of crisp curls that requires very little trimming and needn't be shaved down. Brush and comb through before the bath, and remove any stray longer hairs all over the head and body with scissors. Bathe and don't touch the coat. Allow it to air-dry, unbrushed.

Irish Water Spaniel

The Irish Water Spaniel should have a peaked topknot and a beard left in place. You can shape the topknot with scissors into a peak between the eyes, removing stray or uneven hairs. Shave the face smooth in the direction of hair growth, or scissor to neaten. This breed also has a characteristic "rat tail"—a long, thin tail with very short hair. Curls at the tail base should blend gradually into the tail but shouldn't extend more than about 3 inches (7.5 cm) down the tail. Keep the topknot and ears tangle-free.

Portuguese Water Dog

This breed doesn't shed but grows its hair-coat just like human hair, necessitating regular brushing and haircuts. The Portuguese Water Dog typically sports one of two clips: the Retriever clip, in which it is shaved down to about 1 inch (2.5 cm) all over with the tail tuft left long; or the Lion clip (the clip most often seen in the show ring), in which the hindquarters (except for the tail tip) are clipped short but the forequarters—chest, back, front legs, and head—are left long and wavy or curly, depending on the coat.

The Retriever clip is certainly the easiest to care for. If you choose to keep your Portuguese Water

The Curly-Coated Retriever has a short coat of crisp curls that requires very little trimming and needn't be shaved down.

Dog in a Lion clip, comb or pick out tangles all the way to the skin at least every other day.

THE HERDING BREEDS

The herding breeds include the following:

- Komondor
- Puli

The herding breeds with curly coats are typically allowed to form corded coats. Any longhaired, curly-coated dog has the potential to form cords (like "dreadlocks"), and Poodles were once shown this way, but today the two breeds most known for sporting corded coats are the large white Komondor and the small black Puli.

Corded coats are easy to groom once cords have formed, normally by two years of age. To facilitate cord formation, work out mats and woolly tangles with the fingers so that the coat will cord without matting. Here is how to groom a corded dog.

1. Do not brush or comb out the corded coat!
2. Shave the anal area carefully to 1/2 inch (1.5 cm), and shave the abdomen from groin to naval and down the insides of both thighs.
3. While bathing, use a sponge to work water and then shampoo into the cords. Rinse thoroughly.
4. Squeeze-dry cords with a towel.
5. Trim and neaten frayed ends with scissors.
6. To remove mats, use a mat-splitting comb and reshape cords by hand.

THE CURLY TERRIERS

The curly terriers include the following:

- Bedlington Terrier
- Kerry Blue Terrier

These are uniquely curly terriers with soft coats, so unlike the wirehaired terriers, they don't require stripping. Instead, these breeds are scissored for the show ring, although pets may be clipped with an electric clipper.

Bedlington Terrier

To achieve the Bedlington Terrier's characteristic lamb-like look:

1. Using a #15 blade, shave the face from the front edge of the ears to the outer eye corners and straight down to 1/2 inch (1.5 cm) from the corner of the mouth, including under the jaw, against the direction of hair growth.
2. Shave the back edges of the ears diagonally down to a point at the base of the throat and down to about 2 inches (5 cm) below the Adam's apple in a V-shape.
3. Clip the ears on both sides, leaving a V-shaped tassle at the end of both ears.

Clipping pattern for the Bedlington Terrier

4. Carefully shave the anal area, and shave the underside of the tail about one third of the way down, then shave the rest of the tail on all sides.

5. The rest of the body should be shaved (for pets) or scissored to about 1 inch (2.5 cm) all around.

6. The leg hair should be clipped or scissored to be slightly longer than the body hair. Trim between foot pads and scissor around the feet to emphasize their angular "hare foot" shape.

7. Finally, scissor the topknot of the Bedlington so that it forms a "Roman arch" or "Roman nose" from the base of the neck to the tip of the nose, to achieve the characteristic lamb look.

Kerry Blue Terrier

The Kerry Blue Terrier has an overall shape similar to the Wire Fox Terrier, but the coat is soft and wavy rather than hard and wiry. To groom a Kerry Blue Terrier:

1. Clip the stomach with a #10 blade to about

Clipping pattern for the Kerry Blue Terrier

3 inches (7.5 cm) in front of the back legs. Carefully clip the ears on both sides.

2. On the head, imagine a line from behind the ears to the upper chest and another line from just between the eyes to the hair follicle lump under the chin, shaving under the jaw into a V-shape on the chest that comes to about 2 inches (5 cm) above the breastbone.

3. Comb the beard hair forward and carefully cut the hair around the eyes with scissors.

4. Scissor or shave the body coat to about 1.5 inches (4 cm) with a #5 or #7 blade on the clipper. Trim the tail hair short and shave the anal area. Shave the hair between these lines including the top of the skull, then blend with scissors into the beard and muzzle.

5. Brush leg hair with a slicker brush and trim feet to a cylindrical shape.

6. Finish by top-brushing the coat with a natural bristle brush sprayed with coat conditioner for a nice sheen.

THE NON-SPORTING BREEDS

The non-sporting breeds include the following:
- Bichon Frise
- Poodle (Standard, Miniature, Toy [companion breed])

All Wet

You may notice the term "water" in several of the curly-coated breeds. Indeed, the curly coat is particularly good at insulating and repelling water, and even the Poodle was originally a water retriever, although today he is mostly used as a companion. (Some people even argue that the Poodle should be classified as a sporting breed!) Other breeds, such as the herding and terrier breeds, probably benefited from their curly coats as they worked out in the harsh, wet elements; the curly coats protected against rain, keeping them warm and relatively dry.

Both of these breeds require constant vigilance to keep their ever-growing coats free of mats and tangles. Never bathe a matted Bichon or Poodle. Instead, spray these curly coats with coat conditioner and brush and comb them *every day* to keep them untangled. Treat these coats with care to prevent hair breakage.

Bathe your curly companion every two to four weeks and rinse thoroughly. After towel-drying, blow-dry with a slicker or pin brush, brushing away from the body to achieve a fluffy, powderpuff appearance.

Although the Bichon and Poodle coats are similar in texture, Poodles may be cut into many different styles. Bichons are typically cut into one characteristic style, resembling a powderpuff.

Bichon Frise

To shape the Bichon, think round. Keep eyeing a picture of a well-groomed Bichon as you work, scissoring rather than clipping to shape the coat coat. Here's how.

1. After bathing and fluff-drying, face your Bichon and comb the topknot off the face. Scissor off any hair covering the eyes.
2. Part the hair on the muzzle and scissor off hair blocking vision. Comb muzzle hair down.
3. Scissor the top of the head into a rounded shape, blending head hair into the ears and beard to form a half-moon shape.
4. Neaten but do not shorten the beard.
5. Trim hair under the ears so that the ears fall naturally.
6. Round the head from profile. Keep scissoring to achieve a round shape.
7. Blend chest hair into beard, neck, and head to continue the rounded lines.
8. Scissor the front legs into straight lines from the front, cylindrical from afar.
9. Trim hair between the legs to blend into the bottomline from the side.
10. Trim the topline level, with coat along the back shorter than on the neck.

> The Bichon Frise is a non-sporting breed that requires constant vigilance to keep his constantly growing coat free of mats.

11. Leave tail hair long but neatened and shorten around the anal area.

Poodle (Standard, Miniature, and Toy)

At last we come to the Poodle, the breed most likely to appear in the widest variety of grooming styles. The Poodle's versatile coat suits him for an endless number of clips. He may have a clean, shaved face, a rounded mustache, a squared-off French mustache, and any number of different body styles.

In the show ring, any Poodle under 12 months may be shown in a "Puppy" clip, but all adult Poodles must be shown in either the English Saddle clip or the Continental clip. Pet Poodles are characteristically kept in short, easy-care coats but require clipping about every four weeks.

The fun thing about Poodles is that you can easily try different styles and clips. The coat grows so fast that it lends itself to experimentation. Whether you decide to clip your Poodle yourself or let a professional groomer do it, keep him well brushed and combed between clipper sessions to prevent that curly coat from becoming a mess of mats.

Poodles can be clipped into many different styles. Some of the coat options available include the following:

- Bikini clip
- Continental clip
- Dutch clip
- English saddle clip
- Kennel clip
- Lamb clip
- Miami clip
- New Yorker clip
- Puppy clip
- Retriever clip
- Sporting clip
- Teddy Bear clip
- Town and Country clip

Maintaining a show coat on a Poodle is an awesome task. The topknot and ears are banded and wrapped to keep them clean, and the coat is handled with immaculate care so as not to break the hairs and compromise the coat's quality. For the pet owner, however, a shorter and more sensible clip is much easier to maintain. Even so, keep a picture of the clip you are imitating in front of you so that you can keep checking the shape and comparing it to your work.

Bathe your Poodle every two to four weeks. Then, to groom him at home in a basic Kennel clip:

The fun thing about the Poodle coat is that you can easily try different styles and clips.

POODLE CLIPS

Bikini

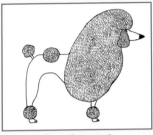

Continental

Dutch

English Saddle

Lamb

Miami

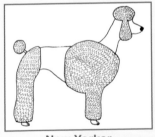

New Yorker

Puppy

Retriever

Sporting

Teddy Bear

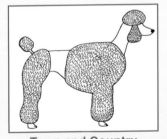

Town and Country

Maintaining a show coat on a Poodle can be a tremendous task.

1. Fluff-dry the coat with a soft slicker brush and a blow-dryer set on low or cool.

2. Shave the face with a #15 blade on an electric clipper. Or leave a doughnut-shaped or French mustache on the muzzle, shaping with scissors.

3. With the same #15 blade, clip the paws on the top, sides, between the toes, and between the pads. This is difficult and must be practiced carefully, especially on Toy Poodles, who have tiny feet. The Poodle is the only breed with feet shaved clean.

4. Clip the tail, leaving a pom-pom (shaped with scissors) on the end of the tail if desired.

5. Shave the body with a #5 blade down the backbone from the base of the neck to the base of the tail, then down each side, including chest and ribs, to about 1/2 inch (1.5 cm) in length. Blend the neck into the coat.

6. Scissor the legs to about 1/2 inch (1.5 cm) in length.

7. Brush and comb out long ear hair, trimming with scissors to neaten.

8. Shape the topknot by scissoring the headpiece into a rounded shape.

9. Next month, experiment with a different clip!

What Your Curly/Wavy Coat Should Look Like

This photo gallery demonstrates what your well-groomed curly- or wavy-haired dog should look like.

American Water Spaniel

Coat: Outercoat varies from uniformly wavy to closely curled and dense; undercoat is weather resistant.
Colors: Dark chocolate, liver, solid brown.
Grooming: Routine brushing and occasional trimming.

Bedlington Terrier

Coat: Crisp, thick, linty, with mixture of hard and soft hair standing away from body; tendency to curl, especially on head and face; topknot.
Colors: Blue, blue and tan, liver, liver and tan, sandy, sandy and tan.
Grooming: Scissor for the show ring; clip about every six weeks for pets.

Bichon Frise

Coat: Outercoat is coarse, curly; undercoat is soft, dense.
Colors: Solid white, shadings permissible.
Grooming: Daily brushing and combing required, as are monthly coat trimmings with scissors.

Curly-Coated Retriever

Coat: Water resistant with small, tight, crisp, close-lying curls.
Colors: Black, liver.
Grooming: Brush and comb.

Irish Water Spaniel

Coat: Abundant hair falls in dense, tight, crisp ringlets or waves.
Color: Solid liver.
Grooming: Regular brushing and combing are essential. Scissoring and shaving are necessary.

Kerry Blue Terrier

Coat: Wavy, soft, silky, dense.
Colors: Any shade of blue-gray or gray-blue; may have small white markings; may have black points.
Grooming: Show dogs require professional grooming to achieve sculpted look. Pets need grooming every six to eight weeks.

Komondor

Coat: Outercoat is long, wavy, curly, coarse; undercoat is soft, woolly; coarser hairs of outercoat trap undercoat, forming strong cords.
Color: White.
Grooming: Cords occur naturally but require special care: hours of blow-drying, hand-separation of cords weekly.

Miniature Poodle

Coat: Curly has naturally harsh texture, dense throughout; corded hangs in tight, even cords of varying length.
Colors: White, cream, brown, apricot, black, blue, silver, gray, café-au-lait.
Grooming: Many clips require professional grooming. Regular brushing necessary.

Portuguese Water Dog

Coat: Curly has compact, cylindrical curls, somewhat lusterless; wavy falls gently in waves, has slight sheen.
Colors: Black, white, brown tones, combinations of black or brown with white.
Grooming: Both coat types need a lot of attention: either shaving or clipping. Wavy coat must be brushed, combed, and trimmed. Curly coat requires regular brushing and combing.

Puli

Coat: Outercoat is weather resistant, long, wavy or curly, coarse; undercoat is fine, soft, dense. Adult coat forms natural cords.

Colors: Solid black, rusty black, all gray shades, white.

Grooming: Cords require occasional separation and trimming.

Standard Poodle

Coat: Curly has naturally harsh texture, dense throughout; corded hangs in tight, even cords of varying length.

Colors: White, cream, brown, apricot, black, blue, silver, gray, café-au-lait.

Grooming: Many clips require professional grooming. Regular brushing necessary.

Toy Poodle

Coat: Curly has naturally harsh texture, dense throughout; corded hangs in tight, even cords of varying length.

Colors: White, cream, brown, apricot, black, blue, silver, gray, café-au-lait.

Grooming: Many clips require professional grooming. Regular brushing necessary.

PART FOUR
GROOMING FOR
SPECIAL NEEDS

12

GROOMING A PUPPY

Puppies may be small—or relatively small—but those squirming, wagging, romping bundles of energy are anything but easy to groom. Puppies love to be on the move, and they may not be particularly thrilled about sitting nicely for a long session of brushing, toenail clipping, and primping. However, because puppies grow—and some grow really big—puppyhood is the best time to establish a regular grooming routine. Just try to trim a full-grown Irish Wolfhound's nails if he doesn't want you to do it. Don't expect to have the upper hand when it comes to physical strength.

Grooming a puppy isn't exactly like grooming an adult dog. Puppy coats are often different than their adult manifestations will be. Long coats haven't reached their full adult length. Other coat types take a while to achieve their adult texture, their double-coated nature, or their mature fullness. Puppies may not need to be groomed as often as adults, but especially for long and curly-coated breeds that will require frequent grooming as adults, getting puppies in the habit now is the best and easiest way to facilitate future grooming sessions.

SOCIALIZE YOUR PUPPY TO GROOMING

Puppies have certain natural tendencies that can make grooming difficult. They may not like their paws handled, they may not be patient enough to stand still for a long detangling session, and they may balk at the handling of their mouths and ears. However, puppies can learn early that grooming is safe, inevitable, and rewarding.

Your puppy is a baby, and just like any young, immature mammal, he must learn things in little steps. You can't expect a 12-week-old Afghan Hound puppy to endure three hours of brushing—and luckily, the Afghan puppy's coat doesn't yet require it. But someday that coat will require long hours of grooming, so baby steps are the key to success.

Begin grooming your puppy as soon as you bring him home, and while you can certainly adapt a grooming schedule to fit your own needs, the one set forth below works well. Don't rush

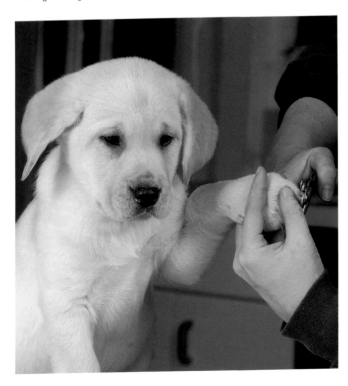

Your puppy should learn to accept grooming in tiny increments; don't rush him through the process.

Keep grooming positive for your puppy by praising him and rewarding him with treats.

Ask the Groomer

Q: What is socialization, exactly?

A: Puppies have certain natural behaviors (barking, jumping, chewing, using the world as their personal toilet) that make socialization and training necessary if they are to live with humans. Training sets up house rules, while socialization is the process of getting a puppy used to lots of different people, other dogs, and diverse situations from a young age so that he becomes a well-adjusted, confident, friendly adult dog. Some trainers recommend introducing a puppy to new people, dogs, and situations every single day of his life for the first year.

anything. Whenever your puppy gets nervous or apprehensive about anything you are doing, stop and take it back a step. Little bits of grooming applied consistently, evolving gradually and comfortably into a full-blown grooming routine, will keep grooming positive for both you and your puppy.

Never underestimate the power of treats when training your puppy to accept grooming. What puppy wouldn't want to sit nicely for grooming if it meant lots of treats? Every grooming session, no matter how old your puppy gets, should end with a treat and praise. However, although early grooming sessions will go more smoothly if you give your puppy lots of small treats throughout, grooming doesn't have to become a treat-dispensing session for every single step. Those early treats help associate the grooming process with rewards in your puppy's mind. Once that connection

During Week 1, pick up each of your puppy's paws and gently handle them to prepare him for nail clipping later.

is established, he will enjoy grooming without constant treats.

Praise is also important. Some puppies, especially those who aren't particularly food motivated or who can't eat very much at once (small breeds especially), may not care to down too many treats. Overfeeding is never healthy, and considering that obesity is the most common health problem in pets according to vets, too many treats are never a good idea. Praise can be just as powerful, if not more powerful, than treats, depending on your dog's personality, but a combination of lots of praise and some strategically offered healthy treats works best for most dogs.

Do each of the following activities with your puppy every day at the same time:

Week 1

1. Pick up each of your puppy's paws. Wiggle his nails and press on his paw pads. Give him lots of praise and a small treat or piece of kibble after each paw.
2. Handle each ear and look in the ear. Praise and treat.
3. Touch your puppy's muzzle. Praise and treat.
4. Look at each eye, stroking his face with your hands. Praise and treat.
5. Lift up and handle the tail, checking the anal area for cleanliness.
6. Stroke his coat with your hand and praise him.
7. Finish with a treat. Wasn't that fun? (Your puppy surely thought so!)

Week 2

1. Continue Week 1 items.
2. Gently take your puppy's muzzle in one hand and insert your fingers in the corners of his mouth. Gently touch a couple of teeth with your finger. Praise and treat.
3. Let your puppy sniff and explore a soft natural bristle brush. Put a treat on the bristles for him to find.
4. Let your puppy sniff and explore a nail clipper appropriately sized for him. Praise and offer a treat.

Beauty Tip

Big, fattening, artificially colored and flavored, preservative-filled treats aren't good for any dog. To combat obesity and encourage good health, many trainers prefer to use bits of a puppy's regular kibble as a treat. Take kibble from your puppy's regular dietary allowance rather than adding additional kibble. For example, if your puppy usually gets 1 cup of kibble a day, feed 3/4 cup for meals (divided into two or three meals), and reserve 1/4 cup for treats to use in grooming and training. Every bite counts, especially for toy dogs, who can easily become overweight with just a few extra calories each day. Or try healthy "people food" as a treat: slices of raw baby carrots, blueberries, or tiny broccoli florets. Every now and then, bits of cheese and meat make treats interesting and enjoyable, in addition to adding nutrients. Avoid any treats with artificial colors, flavors, preservatives, and sugar.

Week 3

1. Continue Week 1 items.
2. Open your puppy's mouth and rub his teeth briefly with a soft cloth. Examine his teeth and gums. Try to stop *before* he begins to resist.
3. Gently brush your puppy's coat for a few seconds, then praise and treat.
4. Touch the nail clippers against his paw. If he reacts positively, clip off just the very tip of one or two nails. Praise and treat.

Week 4

1. Continue Week 1 items.
2. Let your puppy explore a toothbrush, sniffing and even chewing it a bit. Praise and treat.
3. Put a little toothpaste made for dogs on your finger and allow him to lick it off. (Don't force it. If he doesn't like it, that's fine. The point is to get him used to the taste, not necessarily to want to gobble it up.)
4. Brush the coat more thoroughly, praising as you go.
5. Clip off any toenail tips you didn't clip last week—just one or two per day.

Week 5

1. Continue Week 1 items.
2. Touch the toothbrush against your puppy's teeth, scrubbing just a little if he responds well. Praise and treat.
3. Brush the coat, then introduce your puppy to a comb. Let him sniff it and touch it on his coat, combing a little if he responds well.
4. Keep handling the paws, monitoring them daily, and snipping off the nail tips when necessary. Don't forget to keep the praise flowing.

Week 6

1. Continue Week 1 items.
2. Brush your puppy's teeth briefly. Praise.

3. Brush and comb the coat.

4. Continue to handle the paws, ears, eyes, tail, and teeth. Be careful handling the mouth when your puppy starts teething. Do not brush the teeth during this time, as his mouth is extra sensitive.

> Your puppy should be well socialized to the grooming process by the sixth week of desensitization.

5. Enjoy your well-behaved and well-groomed puppy!

Beyond Week 6

Your puppy should be well socialized to the grooming process by the sixth week. But don't let that be a reason to slack off. Grooming should be a lifelong process, and a little bit every day for life will train your pet to both accept and enjoy the process.

It's easy to take a well-behaved puppy for granted. If grooming sessions become easy, don't let that be an excuse to stop making them fun. Your puppy may begin to backslide, losing interest and patience in grooming, if you start grooming haphazardly or distractedly or forgetting to praise and reinforce him for good behavior.

Brush Up On a Breed

The Poodle experiences a dramatic coat change somewhere around his first birthday, with great changes in both length and thickness.

BOND WITH YOUR PUPPY

The daily grooming session does more than teach your puppy how to let you maintain his hygiene. It also allows for built-in one-on-one time for the two of you, something crucial to your relationship now and in the future.

It's easy to get busy with daily life and forget to spend time with your puppy. Sure, everyone spends time yelling "No!" and taking the puppy outside when housetraining seems the central focus of the relationship. After that, it's common to walk that dog and pet him absentmindedly while watching television, but many owners never really spend "quality time" with their pets. No, quality time isn't just for human children—dogs benefit from it too.

When you groom your pet, you are focusing all your attention on him. Talk to him, praise him, give him treats, tell him he is a good dog, and teach him how to let you handle his paws, face, ears, and coat. He will learn that he is important to you and that you notice and value him. He will begin to see you as the trusted "pack leader," and his loyalty and devotion will develop quickly. Let grooming time become bonding time and you've accomplished two very important tasks of pet ownership in one short session per day.

ADDRESS SETBACKS

Every puppy has setbacks, and every groomer has stories to tell about the Great Dane puppy who was so patient with grooming and then one day

If your puppy has a grooming setback, don't get frustrated and take it out on him—just be patient and progress slowly and steadily.

suddenly refused to let anyone touch his nails ever again, or the one about the Poodle who wouldn't be seen within a mile of a clipper, or the Shih Tzu who decided he had experienced his very last de-matting session.

Setbacks can occur due to "user error"— clipping the quick on a nail, pulling too hard to untangle a coat, or surprising the dog with an electric clipper before he was prepared. Sometimes, however, setbacks occur for no discernible reason. A puppy is suddenly shy of the scissors, the nail grinder, or even the bathtub and you have no idea why.

When setbacks occur, back up. Take your dog back to the beginning and start over. If he suddenly

If a groomer setback occurs—such as clipping the quick on a nail—start the entire process over again.

fears nail clipping, go back to that very first stage when you let your dog explore the nail clippers without actually clipping the nails, rewarding all the while with praise, reassurance, and the occasional treat. Introduce the clipper back, slowly, as if you were socializing him to nail clipping for the very first time. Do the same thing with the scissors, clippers, comb, or whatever else your dog balks at. Remember to progress again slowly, with lots of rewards, keeping the experience positive, especially if your dog has had reason to associate grooming with a negative experience. You now have the job of replacing that negative experience with positive experiences again.

Whatever you do, when your dog has a grooming setback, don't get frustrated and take it out on him. Dogs don't suddenly resist nail trimming, clipping, or bathing to annoy you. They resist it because they have a reason to resist it. Something happened—whether or not you know about it or see it from your dog's point of view—to cause him to fear or resist some aspect of grooming. Blaming him won't help the situation. Patience, consistency, and slow but steady progress will bring you both back to your once-happy grooming routine again.

KNOW YOUR DOG

Every dog is an individual, and knowing how fast you can progress with grooming is a matter of paying attention to the cues your dog delivers. Some tend to adapt quickly to grooming, while others are particularly shy of grooming tools, especially electronic ones. Cowering, whimpering, backing away, urination, or running away are all signs that your shy, sensitive, submissive, or extra-cautious dog is scared or just a little wary of a tool or a grooming process. If this happens, back up and take it extra slow. If your confident dog has no problem with a nail clipping and

thorough brushing and combing in that first week, that's fine too. It's all a matter of adapting to the needs of your dog's individual personality.

BE PREPARED

Some puppy coats morph pretty subtly into their adult versions, but some come into their adult coats in a rather dramatic fashion involving tons of hair loss, a temporarily patchy coat, and the development of an undercoat more dramatic and challenging than any the puppy owner had imagined. Some pet owners give up on grooming their pets once that adult coat finally comes in. Suddenly, tangles form daily where once they were infrequent.

Knowing that a coat change is in the works for your puppy can help you be prepared. Also remember that when he "blows coat" for the first time, losing his puppy coat and growing in his full, thick adult coat, the heavy-duty grooming chores related to the dropped coat won't last forever and will typically occur only once or twice a year. Just keep brushing, combing, brushing, and bonding!

13

FLEA AND TICK PREVENTION AND TREATMENT

Maybe your dog will be one of the lucky ones who never gets fleas, but don't put money on it! Fleas aren't just for stray dogs. Even the most pampered pet can get fleas on a walk or out in the yard. If a dog in the neighborhood or at a dog show has fleas, all pets in the area are at risk. And any dog who ever walks under a tree or through a wooded area is also at risk for ticks.

The diseases that fleas and ticks carry can threaten the health and even the life of your pet. Anemia, flea allergy dermatitis (FAD), Lyme disease, Rocky Mountain spotted fever, and tapeworms are just a sampling of the potential hazards from parasites, so protecting your pet from these pests is more important now than ever before.

Fortunately, many products are available today to fight fleas and ticks. From natural botanicals to the latest in adulticides (which kill adult fleas and ticks), repellents, and various types of insect growth

Good grooming establishes the foundation for pest control.

regulators and related substances that keep flea eggs from hatching or that even dissolve the shells of fleas and ticks, pest control is advanced and continues to advance every year.

Only you can determine how you want to handle pest control for your pet, but this chapter will give you the background and strategies you need to make the right choice for your individual situation.

GROOMING = PEST CONTROL

Good grooming establishes the foundation for pest control because a healthy, well-examined coat and strong, healthy skin will help minimize fleas and help you spot ticks. Pests are naturally attracted to weak animals with vulnerable skin. Of

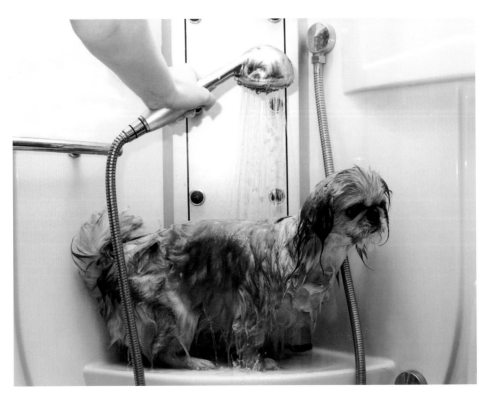

course, where fleas are prevalent, they will jump onto any host they can find (even humans), but if they have a choice, they will usually infest the less healthy hosts.

A healthy diet and good skin and coat care not only help discourage a flea or tick infestation but could help minimize skin reactions to flea and tick bites when they happen. A daily grooming session is also

> A healthy diet can help discourage a flea or tick infestation.

important, especially during flea and tick season. A visual inspection for ticks and a once-over with a flea comb and careful examination for signs of infestation can alert you to the presence of even a couple of fleas before they have a chance to multiply.

Ask the Groomer

Q: Are all pest control products safe for my puppy?

A: Not all pest control products are designed for puppies. Always read the directions and check with your vet if you are unsure about whether your pest control product of choice is safe for your puppy and appropriate for his age and weight.

THE PRICE OF PESTS

Fleas and ticks are more than an inconvenience. They can cause serious health problems for your beloved pet. Here is a rundown of what can happen if your dog develops a pest-related health problem.

From Hot Spots to Hives

Flea and tick bites can irritate even the healthiest of dogs, and dogs with sensitive skin may develop agonizing allergic reactions to flea and tick bites. From flea allergies to fleabite dermatitis, fleas make skin itch. When a dog scratches and licks at one spot too much, the area can become inflamed and infected—resulting in what's called a "hot spot." Allergic reactions to flea and tick bites can result in rashes, hives, hair loss, and chronic irritation.

Constant skin irritation can compromise your dog's quality of life, so stop it before it starts, and if he develops a skin irritation or allergy from pests, don't ignore it. See your vet and treat it right away, before it gets worse. Your dog has much better things to do than scratch his life away.

Pest-Borne Diseases

Both fleas and ticks can transmit many diseases to your pet through their bites. The following are some of the flea and tick diseases that affect dogs.

1. Anemia is a disease that can be caused by the bloodsucking flea, resulting in symptoms of tiredness and general weakness.
2. Canine ehrlichiosis, contracted from the common brown dog tick, occurs mainly in the Gulf Coast area, the Eastern seaboard, the Midwest, and California.
3. Lyme disease, the most common tick-borne illness in the United States (occurring mainly in the Northeast, upper Midwest, northern California, and the Pacific Northwest), occurs when a tick bites a dog and stays attached for at least 5 to 20 hours. Humans can also contract Lyme disease from ticks.
4. Rocky Mountain spotted fever can be contracted from several tick species; humans can also catch this disease (occurring mainly in the southeastern United States, the Midwest,

Plains states, and the Southwest).
5. Tapeworms, evident via 1/4-inch-long (.5-cm) egg-filled body segments in a dog's feces or around the anal area, are transmitted to dogs through fleabites.

Now let's take a look at fleas and ticks more closely and see what you can do to eradicate and prevent these pests.

FLEAS

How do you know if fleas are present? They leave telltale signs, such as:

- flea dirt (digested blood), which looks like tiny reddish brown specks
- flea eggs, which look like tiny white specks
- actual fleas, which are brown, about 2 millimeters long, and crawl or jump
- itching—although dogs can itch for many reasons, itching and subsequent scratching

Beauty Tip

Old-fashioned flea powders, sprays, dips, and flea collars contain chemicals that must be handled with extreme caution. Preferable are spot-on preparations, which are easy to use and are applied monthly between the pet's shoulder blades and also at the tail base for larger dogs. These chemicals are generally safe for most pets if you follow package directions precisely, but some pets react negatively to these spot-on products. Talk to your vet about which products she recommends as safest and most effective for your pet, as there is a variety available for prevention and treatment.

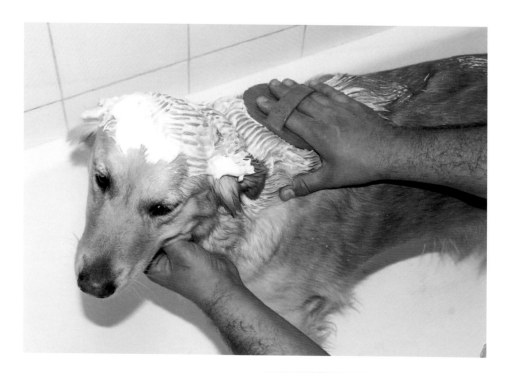

are often caused by fleas, especially during warm weather

How to Eliminate Fleas

For minor pest occurrences, you may not need to do anything more than bathe your dog frequently and use the flea comb diligently. Bathing drowns fleas. You don't even need to use chemicals, although a natural botanical flea dip or shampoo can help repel pests and condition your pet's skin. For dogs who spend time outside, bathe weekly during flea season and finish every grooming session by running through every last bit of your dog's coat with a fine-toothed comb, no matter the coat length.

Flea combs remove fleas because the teeth are so close together that they lift the flea from the coat. A daily comb-through with the flea comb between weekly baths will keep many dogs flea-free. However, if more than a flea or two continues to be present daily for more than a week or if your dog is sensitive to fleabites, consider using a chemical flea control product. Talk to your vet about your best options.

Here's a step-by-step way to rid your dog of fleas, no products required:

1. Bathe your dog in a bathtub or tub of water. Instead of letting the water drain, let the tub fill. Scrub the coat well, all the way down to the skin, especially around the ears, tail, and abdomen, where fleas tend to congregate.

2. Have your dog sit in the bathwater to drown

> For minor pest occurrences, one of the things you can do is bathe your dog frequently, which drowns fleas.

After shampooing your dog to rid him of fleas, rinse the coat thoroughly for five minutes.

fleas in the tail area as you scrub the rest of the coat.

3. Rinse the coat thoroughly for five minutes, continuously spraying with a handheld sprayer or pouring clean water from a cup over the entire coat. (Protect the ears from getting water in them by plugging them with cotton balls or holding the ear, folded over, during rinsing.)

4. Dry as you would normally.

5. Finally, with a flea comb or your dog's regular fine-toothed comb, work slowly over his coat from tail to head. Make sure that you comb all the way down to the skin.

6. If any fleas, flea dirt, or flea eggs remain, you'll find them. Drop fleas in a small amount of rubbing alcohol to kill them as you go, then flush them when you are done. You probably won't be able to kill them by squeezing them between your fingers because of their hard shells.

7. If you don't find any fleas after the thorough bath, great! However, repeat the flea combing process daily and bathe weekly to keep them at bay.

Flea Prevention

For some pets and some environments, bathing and flea combs are not enough. Instead, you need a multi-pronged approach: Treat the pet, the house, and in some cases, even the yard. Because there are so many pest control products available, you must decide which kinds you want to use on your pet.

If you are uncomfortable with using the chemicals in flea control products, many of which are neurotoxins, you may decide to use organic products made from natural botanicals and other nontoxic substances. These products don't work as quickly or as thoroughly as mainstream flea and tick control products, but they pose less risk to the pet due to product toxicity or misuse, and they may be just fine for minor pest problems. For serious pest problems or in areas where fleas and/or ticks are a persistent problem, the most effective product is probably a spot-on product, applied monthly, available from your veterinarian.

Before the advent of spot-ons, which are highly effective at completely controlling fleas in many cases, much more environmental

treatment was necessary than it is today. Carpet sprays and powders, room foggers, and yard sprays were once necessary to get a handle on fleas. Still, during flea season you can help minimize the chances of a flea infestation by vacuuming frequently (especially areas frequented by your dog), and in severe cases, sprinkling carpets and furniture with a flea control product

made for this purpose. (The nontoxic varieties are safest and can be very effective when used in combination with a spot-on product.)

Some spot-ons also protect against ticks and/or mosquitoes, so use according to exposure risk.

TICKS

How do you know if your dog has a tick? Ticks are evident by their presence. They can range from pinhead-sized to pea-sized, but when they attach and fill with blood, they can become as large as marbles. You may find them crawling on your dog or attached with their head buried in his skin.

How to Remove a Tick

Ticks can transmit a variety of infectious diseases to both dogs and humans, so remove them with

Pesticide Caution

Always read directions carefully when using any pesticide for any reason, especially if you have young children. Never use a dog flea product on a cat or vice versa, and always apply the correct dosage at the correct frequency. Talk to your vet if you suspect that you may have misused a pesticide or if your pet experiences any health problems after using a pesticide product, such as a rash, hair loss, itching, lethargy, seizures, loss of motor function, or collapse.

Ticks can transmit a variety of infectious diseases to both dogs and humans.

caution. Never touch a tick, especially one that's blood filled, with your bare hands—the bacteria in the tick's blood could infect you. Also, never pull out a tick with its head buried in your dog's skin or the wound could become infected. Instead, remove a tick like this:

Check your dog for fleas and ticks after he's been playing outdoors.

1. Using a cotton ball, wet the tick with nail polish remover or rubbing alcohol, or with a tick spray available at pet stores.
2. Wait for a few minutes or until the tick begins to pull out of the skin.
3. Wearing surgical gloves or holding a paper towel, or using tweezers or a special tick-removing tool, lift the tick off your dog.
4. Drop the tick in a small amount of rubbing alcohol. When it is dead, flush it down the toilet.

If the tick's body comes out but his head remains embedded in your dog, take your dog to the vet.

Tick Prevention

Just as with fleas, prevention is your best option. Protect your dog with a tick collar or topical medication. Ask your vet which products she recommends for your individual dog. Also, inspect him after he has been playing outside and groom him regularly.

14

SENSITIVE SKIN CARE

A dog's skin is one of his most sensitive and easily damaged organs. Although dogs tolerate puppy biting in the whelping box better than we humans tolerate those needle teeth on our hands, dog skin is actually thin and more prone to problems than human skin. If a dog develops a skin problem—an allergy, a wound, or a reaction to a fleabite, for example—it can initiate a cycle of skin problems that can be very difficult to resolve. For this reason, home groomers must take extra care not to aggravate a dog's skin with a hot pair of clippers, poorly aimed scissors, or too-rigorous brushing with the sharp wire bristles of a slicker brush.

Some breeds in particular have extra-sensitive skin and may react to things other breeds would tolerate without a problem. For each individual dog, there is a line between frequent grooming to stimulate the skin and coat, to keep it healthy, to distribute coat oils, and to remove tangles, and overgrooming to the point of aggravating the skin.

Every dog can be brushed and combed daily, but some dogs may need a softer brush or a gentler touch. If your dog has sensitive skin, this chapter is for you, but even pet owners whose dogs seem to have tough, resilient skin can benefit from a little extra caution. Once an irritated skin cycle begins, it can

A dog's skin is thin and more prone to problems than human skin.

be hard to stop, and you can't reason with a dog about why he shouldn't scratch and lick that itchy, sore spot.

SENSITIVE SKIN: WHO HAS IT?

Any dog can have sensitive skin, but some breeds tend to have sensitive skin more than others. If your dog has a white or light-colored coat and pink skin or a very sparse coat or no coat, he may be more sensitive to everything: dry air, wind, sun, and irritation from products such as shampoos, conditioners, and coat sprays. Some breeds that may tend to have more sensitive skin, ranging from allergies to sunburn risk to skin fold dermatitis, include the following:

- Afghan Hound
- Basset Hound

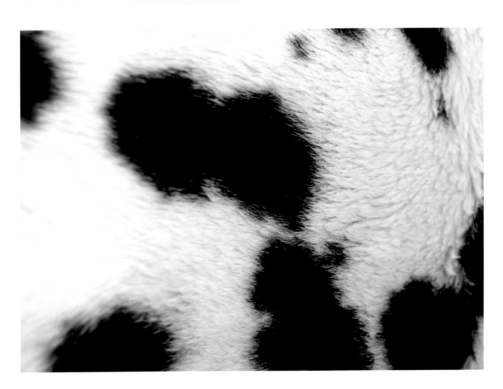

- Bichon Frise
- Boston Terrier
- Bulldog
- Chinese Crested
- Chinese Shar-Pei
- Cocker Spaniel
- Dalmatian
- English Springer Spaniel
- French Bulldog
- Golden Retriever
- Great Pyrenees
- Italian Greyhound
- Komondor
- Labrador Retriever (yellow)
- Manchester Terrier
- Pekingese
- Pembroke Welsh Corgi
- Poodle (white)
- Pug
- Saint Bernard
- Saluki
- Tibetan Terrier
- West Highland White Terrier
- Whippet

That's not to say that every pink-skinned or light-coated individual will have sensitive skin or that your black Lab *won't* have sensitive skin. An injury or a flea infestation can cause any dog to develop skin problems. But for those breeds with sensitive skin, take extra care to proceed with grooming gently so as not to aggravate the skin.

SPECIAL CONCERNS FOR SENSITIVE SKIN GROOMING

When grooming any dog, take care not to injure the skin. Slicker brushes, clippers, and scissors are all potentially injurious to a dog's skin. For dogs with sensitive skin, use tools lightly and take special care when grooming a canine with skin problems.

Skin problems are for a vet to address, and a groomer shouldn't try to "fix" these issues, but grooming can certainly prevent some of these problems. Skin disorders that can be caused by or aggravated by grooming include the following:

Allergies

Many dogs develop allergies from food, external

The Saluki is one of the breeds known for having sensitive skin.

environmental sources, or inhaled substances. In dogs, allergies are most likely to manifest on the skin. The most common type of allergy in dogs is flea allergy dermatitis (FAD), an allergic reaction to flea saliva. Allergies can develop as rashes, hives, and/or severe itching. Don't brush over rashes or hives. If hair is tangled, work through it gently with a comb.

Allergies can develop as rashes, hives, and/or severe itching.

Allergies can trigger a vicious cycle—they cause itching, which causes scratching and licking, which causes more irritation. Even after fleas are eliminated, the negative effects on a dog's skin can last for months. Always address allergic reactions with a veterinarian, who can advise you about how to groom hair over these areas.

Brush Burn and Clipper Burn

These skin conditions are a direct result of grooming. Brush burn is caused by brushing too hard, damaging the skin. Clipper burn is a result of allowing a clipper to become too hot (this happens with extended use), burning the dog. Not only can such grooming mishaps be prevented, but when they occur, they can also make future grooming sessions extremely difficult. Dogs remember!

Always brush gently, especially with a wire slicker brush (or even a pin brush), which can be sharp. Short, gentle strokes are better than long, hard ones to work out tangles. When brushing vigorously down to the skin, use a natural bristle brush and save the slicker brush for working out mats.

Turn off the clipper frequently during grooming, have spare blades handy when the blades you are using get too hot, or use a cooling spray for your clipper. Touch the clipper blade frequently to make sure that it isn't too hot. Never run clippers over sensitive areas like the chin and neck more than twice, especially when using a #10 or #15 blade.

Hot Spots

Hot spots are moist, hot wound-like areas that develop quickly and are very painful. They may be caused by a variety of triggers: fleas, allergies, irritants, infections, and even a lack of adequate grooming. Hot spots develop and grow because the dog obsessively licks and scratches at the itchy, painful spots, making them progressively worse until they become infected. Vets must treat hot spots and will clip hair away to disinfect and treat the area. The dog will probably be treated for itching and may have to wear an inverted cone-shaped device called an "Elizabethan collar" to prevent irritating the spots while they heal.

Parasitic and Fungal Conditions

Fleas and ticks aren't the only creatures that can infect your dog's skin. A fungus can cause ringworm, and a variety of different mites can infect your dog with different kinds of mange. Parasitic and fungal conditions must be treated with vet-prescribed medication.

Product Reactions

Some dogs are sensitive to certain products like shampoos, conditioners, coat sprays, or flea and/or tick control products. If your dog has an unexplained skin reaction, check if you've recently

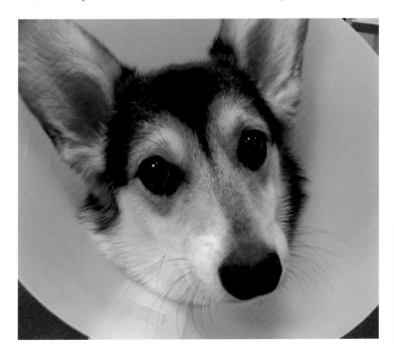

A dog with a hot spot may have to wear an inverted cone-shaped device called an "Elizabethan collar" to prevent irritating the spot while it heals.

One of the most treacherous of grooming activities is scissoring, which is required to maintain the coat shape of some breeds, such as the Poodle and Bichon Frise. This can mean relatively long sessions with sharp scissors next to your dog's sensitive skin. Always pay attention when scissoring your dog, and don't turn on the television or have people in the room distracting you. Keep the scissors pointed down, and always err on the side of scissoring too far from the skin rather than too near. It's too easy to miss and cause a laceration—many dogs have visited the vet to have a scissors slice sutured! Even a professional groomer can get distracted and accidentally nick a dog, and a painful event like this can turn your dog off grooming for good, so be careful.

changed grooming products or food. For dogs with sensitive skin, mild, hypoallergenic, and/or natural products containing skin-soothing ingredients are good to try. Get a product recommendation from your vet if you are unsure.

Skin Diseases

Dogs can develop many different skin diseases, some inherited and some caused by environmental factors. Your vet should always address skin diseases in your dog and can advise you how to groom around them. Whether relatively minor but inconvenient, such as greasy, scaly skin resulting from overactive sebaceous glands (called oily seborrhea), something cosmetic like a disease that causes hair loss (like color mutant alopecia), or something potentially life-threatening like skin cancer, skin disease in dogs must be treated, so please see your vet.

Skin Infections

Skin infections can be caused by bacteria introduced into a wound, by unsanitary conditions, or by poor grooming. From impetigo (a disease causing pustules, common in puppies) to skinfold pyoderma (pus-filled lesions common in loose-skinned breeds like Chinese Shar-Pei) to abscesses of undetermined origin, skin infections should be treated with antibiotics, which your vet can prescribe. Never groom over an infected area. Hair should be cut or carefully clipped from the area so that the infection can heal, but let your vet take care of this procedure.

Sunburn

Dogs can get sunburned, just like people—and they can develop skin cancer too. You can buy sunscreen for dogs in spray form, and this is especially important for hairless, sparsely coated, and light-colored dogs and for all light-colored noses. A human sunscreen recommended by your vet can work if your dog won't lick it off, but just to be safe, a nontoxic sunscreen made for dogs is your best choice. Light-colored dogs who will be outside in sunny weather for more than a few minutes should wear sunscreen, and if you take

Sunburn is a concern for dogs, especially those who are light colored, sparsely coated, or hairless.

your dog to the beach, reapply sunscreen just as you would reapply it to yourself.

NATURAL PRODUCTS FOR GENTLE SKIN CARE

Many pet owners whose pets have sensitive skin have searched and searched for products that work but aren't irritating, and many of these people have finally settled on natural products. Natural products tend to be based on natural botanicals rather than chemicals. They use plant extracts that tend to be soothing and healing to the skin. However, just because something is called "natural" doesn't mean that your dog will necessarily respond well to it. Some dogs have skin reactions to some natural products, but in general, these products are formulated with sensitive skin in mind.

Some of the ingredients in natural products (shampoos, conditioners, coat sprays, and pest control products) that work with canine skin to keep it healthy and free from irritation include natural oils, aloe vera, menthol and/or eucalyptus oil to combat itching, and garlic (a natural antibiotic). Every company has its own unique formula, so get a veterinary recommendation. You may have to try several products before finding one that works well for your pet.

Ask the Groomer

Q: What is an Elizabethan collar?

A: The "Elizabethan collar" is a large, round, plastic, cone-shaped collar that surrounds a dog's head so that he can't lick or bite his skin. Although most dogs don't enjoy wearing this device, it is sometimes necessary when they can't help irritating a wound or other skin problem.

15

DOWN TO THE MAT

A matted coat is a challenge for any groomer, amateur or professional. Mats are solid masses of hair so knotted that they can't be combed out. A matted coat is detrimental to dogs, not only because it looks bad and ruins the coat but also because it can trap moisture, dirt, and bacteria, compromising the health of your dog's skin and even resulting in sores and infections.

A badly matted dog may have suffered grooming neglect, but the presence of a mat doesn't necessarily indicate a lack of good grooming. True, dogs with long, double, or curly coats can develop mats and consequential skin problems when they aren't kept properly brushed and combed, but some breeds develop mats so easily that even with a daily comb-through, a few mats are inevitable here and there, now and then. The trick is to prevent them whenever possible and to know what to do when you encounter them.

Dogs should be tangle-free all the

> A mat is a tangle of hair, often with undercoat, that has formed a knot tight enough to resist brushing and combing.

way down to the skin, so if you do find a mat or two on your dog, this chapter will help you get it out and reclaim his healthy, beautiful, snarl-free coat.

THE MECHANICS OF A MAT

A mat is simply a tangle of hair, often with undercoat, that has formed a knot tight enough to resist brushing and combing. Mats tend to form on dogs with thick, long, curly, or double coats in body "corners" and areas with longer hair, such as the base of the legs, the anal area under the tail, under the chest by the front legs, and around the ears. In most cases, daily brushing and combing will prevent tangles from turning into mats, but sometimes a mat will surprise you.

Mats form because hair is covered in tiny scales, and when hair is unkempt or harshly treated, those scales can stick up, acting like tiny barbs. These barbs catch shed hairs, woolly undercoat hairs, and even dirt and debris, knotting and tangling until they form a solid mass of hair that is virtually impossible to comb through.

Some people tackle mats by cutting them out, which leaves "holes" in the coat, or by shaving the coat all the way off. In severe cases, shaving the coat may be necessary. Regular grooming should preclude this, but if you've let things go, a shave-down-and-start-over approach might be preferable to hours and hours with a mat splitter, scissors, and comb pulling on the poor dog's coat.

If, however, you have just a few mats and want to save that long and lovely coat, try the techniques explained below.

TOOLS

The first step in mat removal is to have the right tools. You may be able to get through most mats with sharp scissors and a comb, but you may also be able to preserve more coat with some specialized equipment and products.

- **Oil-based coat conditioner spray:** Never try to remove a mat without first spraying it with an oil-based coat spray. The oil in this spray smooths down the scales on the hair, essentially taming the "barbs" so that the mat comes out more easily. It saturates and loosens the mat.
- **Mat comb:** A mat comb is a kind of comb-like tool with blades instead of teeth used for slicing large mats into small sections that can then be worked out individually.
- **Mat splitter:** A mat splitter is a blade with a curved handle, used to cut through a mat. The curved handle makes the mat splitter easy to hold and easy to slit into the mat.
- **Sharp scissors:** Sometimes the best way to get through a mat is to cut it into strips. Sharp scissors can do the work of a mat comb or a mat splitter. Always use scissors with extreme care, however, to prevent cutting your dog's skin.
- **Slicker brush:** After cutting the mat into smaller parts, work out the tangles with a slicker brush.
- **Steel comb:** After cutting through a mat and brushing out the tangles, work through the entire area down to the skin, working the smaller tangles out with a fine-toothed comb.

Sometimes the best way to get through a mat is to cut it into strips with sharp scissors.

HOW TO REMOVE A MAT

Once you have the right tools in front of you, you can tackle a mat head-on. Here's how:

Keeping some pets mat-free can be a real challenge.

1. Soak the mat with the oil-based coat conditioner spray. Let the spray penetrate the mat for a few moments to help loosen it.
2. Starting at the outer edge of the mat, try to pick the mat apart with a comb, pulling a few hairs loose at a time with the comb and your fingers. You can also use the pick end of a comb (or even a knitting needle) to try to loosen and pull out the mat.
3. If the mat is still too tight and too large to work through with a comb, use a mat comb to saw the mat into several smaller sections.
4. If the mat is smaller, slice through it with a mat splitter.
5. If you decide to use scissors, be very careful. Dog skin isn't attached to the muscle in the same way human skin is, and it can easily tent

Brush Up On a Breed

Mats sometimes form when a dog is "blowing coat," that approximately annual or biannual period when shedding is particularly heavy. A dog dropping big tufts of undercoat—like the rough Collie—that catch in the longer, harder outercoat can form mats in a single day; so can a puppy dropping his juvenile coat and growing in his adult coat.

up as you pull up hair. It's easy to accidentally slice a dog's skin while trying to cut through a mat. For safety, slide the comb against the skin between the skin and the mat, then cut through the mat over the comb, holding the scissors perpendicular to the comb.

6. Once the mat is cut into smaller pieces, gently brush the pieces out with a slicker brush.

7. Finally, finish with a fine-toothed comb to make sure that the entire mat is gone.

8. Follow up by brushing and combing daily.

Keeping some pets mat-free is a real challenge, but remember that your job is to keep your pet healthy, and that includes his skin and coat. If mat removal and constant grooming really aren't for you, you have three choices: Pay a professional groomer, keep your pet clipped short, or choose a short-coated breed. Just don't allow him to suffer from a matted coat and the health problems that could easily ensue. Better to have no coat at all than a coat in a pathetic mass of mats!

Ask the Groomer
Q: Are mat removers expensive?

A: You can spend a lot of money on many different mat-removing tools, which can make mat removal a little easier and faster, or you can make do with sharp scissors and a comb. You don't have to spend a lot of money to keep your dog mat-free, especially if you prevent mats in the first place by daily brushing and combing.

If you do enjoy the brushing that long and curly coats require, great! If you find that you are pretty good at removing mats, maybe you have hit upon a new career for yourself. The last section of this book will help to get you started if you think that you might want to become a professional groomer.

Keep your dog clipped short if mats are a problem for you.

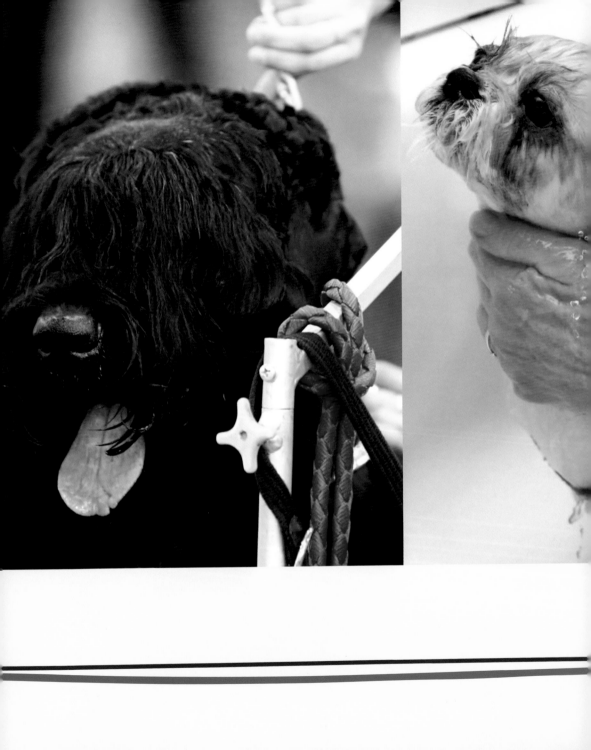

PART FIVE

GETTING STARTED IN

PROFESSIONAL GROOMING

16

IS PROFESSIONAL GROOMING FOR YOU?

Maybe you really enjoy grooming your dog. Maybe you think you're pretty good at it. Maybe friends have been asking for your advice about grooming their dogs or even asking you to do it for them. One person even offered to pay you. Could you have a future as a professional groomer? Professional pet grooming is an exciting career that offers flexibility, independence, and freedom. Grooming dogs is fun, and it can be lucrative too.

However, becoming a professional pet groomer is more than brushing friendly dogs all day. It entails good business planning, patience, people skills, and some pretty rigorous physical labor. This chapter will help you to determine whether you would be willing to accept the kind of life and work necessary for success as a professional pet groomer. Consider each of the questions in terms of your own life, personality, and schedule to get a sense of whether you just like the *idea* of becoming a dog groomer or whether the lifestyle of this flexible and interesting career really would appeal to you.

ARE YOU FULLY INFORMED?

You may have already considered many of the wonderful things about being a professional pet groomer. You get to work with dogs. You get to make dogs look beautiful. You even get to make a dog feel better and enjoy better health by maintaining the grooming so crucial to a healthy coat, skin, and even movement and vision. Many groomers have been the first to spot lumps,

infections, rashes, and other medical problems, and groomers soon learn when to send their clients straight to the veterinarian.

Groomers get to develop relationships with many dogs and get to experience many wonderful dog breeds they couldn't ever own. Those groomers motivated to learn about dogs soon become breed experts, as well as experts in canine health (although good groomers also know when to refer clients to a vet rather than answer crucial health questions on their own).

Self-employed professional groomers get to set their own hours, take on as much or as little work as they like, work at home or in a location of their own choosing, and enjoy the freedom and flexibility of owning a business. Mobile pet groomers get to take their show on the road, perfect for people who don't like to be cooped up inside all day. Even those groomers who are employed at places such as a grooming shop, a pet store, or a veterinary office often get to set their own hours but may enjoy the additional benefits of group employment: insurance, paid vacation, and bonuses.

Perhaps best of all, the professional pet groomer gets to work with animals every day in a helpful, hands-on, interactive environment. Talk about really getting to know dogs! The professional pet groomer knows more about dogs than most people. If you would like to live this kind of life, professional pet grooming may just be for you.

However, pet grooming certainly isn't easy. Sometimes it is hard physical labor. Sometimes it is tedious. Sometimes it's downright dangerous! ("Nice 145-pound [66-kg] doggy…no need to growl like that…just get into this bathtub and let me hose you down.") This is why it's important to consider everything that professional grooming entails before making a final decision.

Beauty Tip

For a vast and comprehensive resource on professional pet grooming, visit www.petgroomer.com. This website seeks to unify professional pet groomers working on their own into a cohesive and communicative whole. From chat boards to grooming contests to everything you ever wanted to know about running a grooming business, this website is a great resource for any professional pet groomer, from beginner to seasoned professional.

ARE YOU MOTIVATED?

Becoming a pet groomer entails good business planning, patience, people skills, and some rigorous physical labor.

One of the reasons many people could never own their own business is motivation. Being your own boss means motivating yourself to get started, finding clients, keeping the schedule, and cleaning up. You can hire people, but then you have to supervise and pay them.

ARE YOU A MULTITASKER?

Operating a business isn't easy, no matter what the business. You have to think about keeping the books, scheduling appointments, and dealing with people. You must keep up with changes and innovations in your field, both health related and tool related. You must keep your shop clean. All this in addition to grooming dogs! As you brush that Beagle, you might need to be planning how to scissor the Bichon, de-mat the Old English Sheepdog, and make a plan for grooming that moppy mixed breed before the afternoon is over.

If you aren't good at handling a lot of different tasks at once, you might not enjoy going into business yourself, let alone this business. Another option is to find a business partner who is good at the things you don't want to handle. While you clip the Poodle and bathe the Schnauzer, your partner can balance the books or greet and schedule customers.

ARE YOU A PEOPLE PERSON?

Dogs may be your business, but if you are a professional groomer, you also have to deal with people. People are your clients and people pay you, so if you don't know how to be pleasant, friendly, communicative, and open, you may find that you have a hard time operating a successful grooming business. People love their dogs and want them groomed by someone with whom they feel comfortable, so if you make people nervous or they think that you aren't friendly, they probably won't want you to groom their dog.

And then there are the people who don't seem to care about their pets at all. You will certainly encounter some people who treat their dogs in a way you won't approve of, from harsh treatment to neglect. As a professional groomer, you can

Groomers get to develop relationships with a variety of dogs.

certainly offer advice, suggesting that a client seek veterinary care or obedience training. However, to stay in business, you must know how to offer advice that can help the dog while remaining polite and nonconfrontational to the customer.

ARE YOU A PLANNER?

Starting a small business takes planning, organization, and decision making. If you can't plan it, it won't happen, and if you can't keep it organized, it will fall apart. Starting a business takes more than confidence and a good idea. It takes foresight.

ARE YOU PATIENT?

Many of the above qualities work hand in hand with patience. Dog grooming is not for people who like to rush through things. You have to enjoy doing a thorough (and that sometimes means *slow*) job on the pets you groom. Sometimes grooming is tedious. Sometimes it is downright monotonous. If you can't handle the occasional (and sometimes frequent) day filled with one dog after another with constant bathing and clipping, or if you find that you don't have the patience to stand and scissor a Poodle or a Bichon Frise to perfection (in fact, if you don't think it's perfectly fascinating!), you might consider a different career course.

ARE YOU SQUEAMISH?

Dog grooming is more than just clipping, trimming, and brushing. It involves dealing with real dogs—dogs who aren't yours and who could come to you with medical problems. You might find infections or sores on a dog you are grooming. You might also sometimes encounter a sick or very nervous dog. If the idea of an occasional encounter with

Refusing Service

As a professional pet groomer, you always have the right to refuse service to anyone or not to groom a dog who represents, in your opinion, an undue risk to you or your employees. Whether a pet owner is rude or a dog seems dangerous, you don't have to take on any client who makes you uncomfortable.

At one point or another, every pet care professional encounters situations in which they believe a pet is at risk or being dangerously mistreated. In such cases, you also have the right to contact the authorities, anonymously if necessary. As a dog professional and an advocate for pets, you may feel that it is your responsibility to report abuse.

To be a successful business owner, you must be pleasant, friendly, and communicative—in other words, a people person.

dog vomit, diarrhea, or even blood sends you screaming in the opposite direction, this may not be the job for you. If the idea doesn't thrill you but you think you can handle it, you may just have the stomach for dog grooming.

ARE YOU STRONG?

Alhough you probably never considered going into physical training for a career as a dog groomer, grooming takes some strength. You may have to lift a large dog onto a table or coax one out of a bathtub. Brushing and combing a large, long-coated dog or clipping a Standard Poodle can really tax your arm muscles, and you may spend hours on your feet. If you aren't in good condition, you may find grooming to be quite taxing.

CAN YOU FOCUS?

Pay attention to anything else when scissoring a dog or clipping a delicate area like the edge of an ear or the anal area and you risk seriously injuring someone's beloved pet. Although every groomer can tell a story about an occasional, accidental nick, grooming absolutely requires focus and full attention to the task. You are using sharp tools around living skin, so if you aren't confident that you can learn to use those tools safely and competently, you might consider another career.

DO YOU HAVE A FEAR OF BEING BITTEN?

You can get insurance to cover yourself in case of a dog bite, but you can't get insurance to prevent a dog bite in the first place. Dealing with other people's dogs automatically entails the risk of a dog bite. Even a well-behaved, nonaggressive dog may bite if he feels fearful, cornered, or startled by new surroundings, new people, and strange tools that buzz, hum, and vibrate.

DO YOU HAVE INVESTMENT CAPITAL?

Even if you open your shop in your own basement, you will need some money to get started.

Ask the Groomer

Q: What are the advantages of mobile pet grooming?

A: Mobile pet grooming is a fun way to work as a professional groomer. Invest in a good van and you can set up a grooming center that travels all around town, offering grooming in the client's own driveway. Many people love the idea of paying for a grooming "house call" rather than having to drive a dog to and from the groomer, and some pets are much more comfortable staying on the premises for their grooming. Mobile pet grooming is also fun because you get to be outside, visit new places, and travel around all day. The scenery constantly changes, and a day on the road in the grooming van can be full of adventure. The cost to purchase the van and the necessary portable equipment can be high, but many mobile groomers claim they are back in the black within a year or two in areas where demand for grooming is high. Mobile groomers can usually charge a little more than home or shop groomers for the convenience of the at-home visit. Research grooming needs in your town and see if it might be the perfect place for a mobile groomer—or another mobile groomer, as many towns and cities already have at least one.

Professional groomers must have high-quality equipment: different types and sizes of brushes, combs,

Grooming requires focus and full attention to the task to prevent injuries.

scissors, clippers with blades, blow-dryers, and cages to keep dogs as they wait to be groomed or to be picked up. You should have a grooming table with a harness and a tub for bathing. The higher quality and more ergonomic these crucial pieces of equipment are, the more they cost. You'll also need a variety of products: shampoos, conditioners, coat sprays, tearstain remover, and flea-control products, not to mention colognes, rubber bands, and a variety of fancy bows and ribbons. And don't forget advertising—that ad in the phone book isn't free.

Eventually, you may even want to include shop rent, decorating expenses, and money to hire and pay employees. All that takes money, so while you can acquire the components for your business a little at a time or all at once, keep in mind that high-quality grooming equipment and supplies aren't cheap. If you don't have the money to spare, you may need to get a small business loan, and then, of course, you have to pay it back (with interest).

ARE YOU BUSINESS-SAVVY?

Opening a grooming business is about much more than grooming dogs. Running a small business, no matter the business, is complicated and takes a lot of knowledge. You can take classes on running a small business, talk to other local business owners, and do a lot of market research, but when it comes down to opening your business, you'll have to put that knowledge into practice or hire someone you trust to do it for you.

The smaller and less formal a grooming practice you have, the less you will have to deal with the ins and outs of running a business, but if you operate

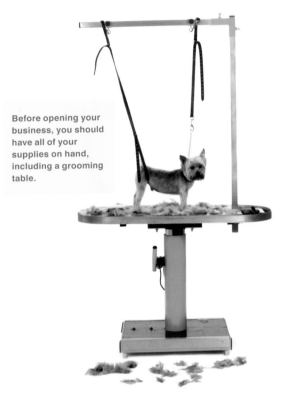

Before opening your business, you should have all of your supplies on hand, including a grooming table.

IS YOUR FAMILY SUPPORTIVE?

No matter how excited you get about becoming a professional pet groomer and/or starting your own business, you must consider how it will affect your family. If you plan to begin grooming dogs at home, will your spouse mind having a house full of strangers, not to mention dog hair? Will you mind having dogs around—dogs who could be unpredictable—if you have young children?

Consider also how your income could change. Some people enjoy an increase in income when they become a pet groomer, but others are willing to accept less income for the increased freedom and enjoyment of this career. Is the rest of your family also willing and able to accept a decrease in income? Having your family behind you can make all the difference in whether or not you have the will, motivation, and confidence to succeed.

ARE YOU WILLING TO KEEP LEARNING?

To be a good groomer is to continue to learn. Styles, techniques, equipment, and products change continually as groomers and manufacturers learn more and as tastes change. The self-employed professional groomer who wants to remain current must make an effort to stay in touch with what is going on in the world

your business for profit (and not just as a hobby), you will need to pay self-employment taxes and file a Schedule C with your income tax form. You'll have to keep track of all your business-related expenses, maintain careful books, and operate your business intelligently. The more you learn about running a business, the more your grooming operation is likely to prosper, so don't forget that although you may have entered into the profession because you love dogs, you need to know a whole lot about business too.

Brush Up On the Stats

According to a recent survey on PetGroomer.com:
- 31% of career grooming seekers were previously employed by the military.
- 71% of career grooming seekers had never worked with pets before.
- 37% of career grooming seekers were between the ages of 25 and 35.

The more you learn about running a business, the more your grooming operation is likely to prosper.

of grooming. Attend classes, seminars, and other grooming events. Attend dog shows often and talk to breeders to learn about the latest in grooming different breeds or about how to groom less common breeds. Ask about products, scissoring techniques, the latest shampoo, and the best way to use the electric clipper on this breed or that.

Joining a professional organization is a great way to keep current on the grooming market, get business advice, and communicate with other groomers to swap hints, tips, and other helpful information. Consider attending a grooming school where you can learn from the professionals.

Everything you do to learn more about grooming will further your career by adding to your knowledge and experience and by giving your clients confidence that you are growing with the field of professional grooming. Plus, the desire to keep learning will keep your interest in grooming piqued. The more you know, the better you will be, and quality is what will keep your clients coming back.

17

HOW TO GET TRAINING

Reading this book is an excellent way to begin a career as a professional groomer, but it is only a first step. Dog grooming is a complex and fascinating subject, and groomers can continue to learn throughout their careers. You can learn about dog grooming by reading lots of books on the subject, talking to groomers, visiting dog shows, and practicing on your own pets and the pets of willing friends. If you are motivated, you can learn quite a bit on your own and can even make a good career for yourself as a professional groomer simply from experience you gain "in the field."

owever, many pet groomers decide to get professional training, often after doing some reading and research on their own. Whether you choose to go it alone or attend a professional school, you can get training from a variety of sources—and sometimes the best and most thorough way is to use as many of them as you can.

CONSIDER GROOMING SCHOOL

Pet grooming schools are popping up all over the country as more and more people express interest in entering this fun profession. Attending a grooming school can give your grooming career a great boost. Many schools teach hands-on grooming of many different breeds, include hundreds of hours of informative courses, and even offer courses on starting and managing your own business. Some schools offer certification, diplomas, and other credits that you can display and use in your advertising after you graduate.

However, not all pet grooming schools are the same or offer the same kinds of classes and credits. Some are geared for more modest career goals like bathing and prep, while others offer more ambitious educational programs, launching you into a truly professional career as a highly skilled groomer. Therefore, don't assume that the pet grooming school nearest you is just as good as the one in a different part of

Many pet groomers decide to get professional training, often after doing some reading and research.

Not all pet grooming schools are the same or offer the same kinds of classes and credits.

the country or is geared toward the goals you have set up for yourself.

Pet groomers often express frustration that more schools don't exist. Sure, it's easier to travel less than an hour to get to school, but the advantages for your future career and income could well depend on which school you choose. If traveling farther means that you'll end up with a better career, you may decide that such an effort and expense is worth it.

But how do you know if grooming school is for you at all? Let's find out.

Do I Really Want to Go to School?

If you are already pretty sure you want to become a professional pet groomer, you may have many of the qualities a successful pet

grooming school student requires: patience, a love of animals, a desire to become a good groomer, and the wish to have a job that offers freedom and flexibility.

However, going to a grooming school also requires some other qualities. Consider the following questions:

- Can you take constructive criticism and learn from it rather than be offended by it? Grooming school teachers are there to help you improve, but you have to be willing to learn from them.
- Do you enjoy learning in a more structured environment, or do you prefer figuring out things on your own?
- Are you willing to learn about business as well as grooming? Are you interested in starting your own grooming shop or getting a job in a shop

or spending with your family—to further your education?

- Have you graduated from high school or the equivalent? Some schools require this.

If grooming school still sounds like a pretty good idea to you, start looking at schools. Here's how.

The Right Grooming School

Good grooming schools aren't available in every state, but even if you live down the road from a grooming school doesn't mean that it's the right one for you. Look around the country at different schools. Ask for their catalogs, look at their websites if they have them, and visit them if you can. Read over the information on each school carefully. Look for signs that the school is reputable, offers quality instruction

owned by someone else? Your preference could determine what kind of school you should attend.

- Can you afford the tuition? Are you willing to take out a student loan? Many schools have loan programs, but not all of them do.
- Can you afford the time to take the classes— time that you can't spend working at another job

If you can, consider as many grooming schools as possible.

by experienced professionals, and has a program that will teach you what you need to know. Here are some questions to consider:

- Is the school state licensed? Is the school accredited?
- How long has the school been in business? What is its reputation? (Ask professional groomers if they have heard of the school.)
- Who are the teachers? What are their credentials? Are the classes actually taught by the teachers advertised in the school materials, or are some classes taught by assistants?
- What are all the costs associated with attending the school, from tuition, books, and equipment to food, lodging, and travel?
- How many hours of instruction are available? Many schools offer basic courses, advanced courses, and professional courses, but compare the hours offered at various schools, which can vary by quite a lot, from 200 to 900 hours of coursework and training for professional-level tracks. Obviously, programs that offer more hours take longer to complete and are usually more extensive, although some shorter-hour tracks are extra intensive. Many of these hours may be "lab" hours of hands-on dog grooming, complemented by lecture hours of classroom learning. Generally, more hours means you'll come out with more experience.
- What diplomas, certifications, or other credentials does the

school award or make available to graduates? How will these credentials translate to the state where you plan to work, if the school is in a different state?
- What percentage of graduates is currently employed as groomers? Does the school keep other records of graduate successes?

Asking questions, doing your research, and extensively comparing different grooming schools are the best ways to figure out which school offers the program and quality you seek. Maybe the

Before choosing a school, find out which certifications and credentials it offers.

school down the road is indeed the perfect school for you, but only after doing your research can you be sure. The more you know about different schools, the more you will have a sense of what makes you comfortable and confident.

When you've finally decided on a school, congratulations! You have some exciting learning to do, and gaining credentials via professional training will give you more information as well as more confidence and experience so that you can best succeed in your new career.

Grooming Correspondence Courses

Many opportunities exist to learn dog grooming via correspondence course. These courses are less expensive and take less time than attending a grooming school. But can you learn how to groom dogs via correspondence? Well, that depends.

Correspondence courses take lots of extra motivation on the part of the student. You have to study the material and watch the demonstration videos without any teacher standing over you or any fellow students to encourage you. You don't gain the same sense of community that you do from a grooming school. You also don't have real dogs to practice on or teachers present to help correct your technique, explain things you don't understand, or guide you in the right direction.

On the other hand, if attending a grooming school isn't an option for you, either due to time or financial constraints, a grooming correspondence course could be just what you need to get you started. If you are willing to get out there and supplement your grooming course with lots of hands-on practice, such as through an apprenticeship with a local professional groomer, you may find this kind of learning experience invaluable.

Correspondence courses are all different, but look for one that gives both grooming information and information on running a small business. The course should also have detailed information on how to groom many different breeds. Compare the cost of the course with grooming schools to get a perspective on whether the price is right, and if possible, get recommendations about the course from others.

Finally, stay motivated to get your money's worth. If you work through all the material, you'll probably gain quite a bit of valuable knowledge.

NETWORK

Whether or not you go to grooming school, networking is extremely important for the grooming professional. Groomers have traditionally been unorganized as a profession, existing in pockets around the country without much communication—until recently. Now that pet grooming is becoming such a popular career,

Network with other professionals to keep up to date on the latest grooming trends and information.

pet groomers are getting organized, with some great results.

One of the primary ways groomers have organized themselves is through professional associations. These associations put on events, share information, and otherwise unite the profession in many productive ways. Some lobby for licensing requirements for groomers (not currently a requirement but available in some states), some conduct meetings or trade shows, and all provide their members with valuable and continually updated relevant information for professional groomers.

Many grooming associations exist on the state level, and a few are national and/

Continually check the Internet for updated grooming information.

or international. Look up grooming associations in your state at the PetGroomer.com website (www.petgroomer.com) for grooming associations, or begin by looking into the currently active national grooming associations. Look in the Resources section of this book for contact information on these grooming associations and more.

BE A SELF-STARTER

The best groomers are self-starters—those rare individuals who get out there and learn without anyone telling them to do it. If grooming truly interests you, you can play a significant part in your own training. The world is filled with great information for groomers. All you have to do is go out and find it. Here are some ideas.

- Read every grooming book you can get your hands on. You'll soon see that some are

more informative than others, some are more specialized or more general than others, and some are aimed more at pet owners. Read them all!

- Continually check the Internet for updated grooming information. Visit PetGroomer.com often, as this site contains links to thousands of grooming-related web pages and is constantly updated. Look around at the personal websites of other groomers too, to get ideas and information.
- Talk to other groomers at every possible opportunity, whether informally or by getting involved with groups like those listed above.
- Commit to continuing education. Attend conferences, educational seminars, and other training sessions.
- Subscribe to pet grooming trade magazines such as *Groom & Board* and *Groomer to Groomer*, as well as pet industry trade magazines that contain grooming sections, such as *Pet Product News*, *Pet Business*, and *Pet Age*.
- Visit dog shows to teach yourself about all the different breeds. Hang around the benching area and talk to the groomers as they do their work

to learn the latest on grooming show dogs. Ask about equipment, products, and the best way to achieve show ring style. (But please be aware that when a dog is about to enter a ring isn't the best time to grill the handler about grooming!)
- Also continue to learn about small business practices if you own your business, even if you operate it from your basement. Take small business seminars and read up on small business operations. Check into local or state laws related to grooming and housing animals.

STAY CURRENT

Although most grooming schools are primarily designed to teach amateur groomers and others with little to no knowledge about pet grooming how to become professionals, many schools also offer courses to keep established and seasoned groomers up to date on the most current trends, tools, and techniques. Even after you have secured employment, don't neglect these opportunities for continuing education.

KNOW YOUR DOGS

In addition to subscribing to grooming and other pet industry publications, pet groomers can benefit from keeping up with general dog magazines that focus on purebred dogs, many of which cover current grooming information. Take a look at *Dog Fancy*, the *AKC Gazette*, *Dog World*, and *Off Lead* magazines. You can learn more than grooming from these magazines; you can learn about the structures, temperaments, strengths, faults, and relevant issues (from legal issues to health issues) of different purebred dogs and of dogs in general. This kind of information can help you keep your finger on the pulse of the dog-owning public, and it can help you better relate to your customers and care for their pets.

18

HOW TO SET UP YOUR OWN BUSINESS

You're trained, you've practiced, and you've decided that you want to open your own grooming business. Or do you? Setting up your own business and joining the ranks of the self-employed may sound glamorous, but it takes a lot of planning, preparation, and (you guessed it) money. Maybe you have a small stash put away to help launch your in-home business, or maybe you plan to get a bank loan, rent a shop, and buy all-new, state-of-the-art equipment. Both routes take planning and some serious consideration about how you will set up, operate, and eventually grow your business.

Although setting up your business will be more or less complex depending on what kind of enterprise you are planning—grooming the pets of friends in your garage or basement is much less of an undertaking than opening up your own shop in a separate retail space—any self-employment will be more profitable, not to mention more enjoyable, if you have a plan and cover all your bases. This chapter will help you consider some of the things involved in setting up your own pet grooming business.

WRITE A BUSINESS PLAN

A business plan is essential for anybody planning to take out a business loan. A bank may or may not want to see one, but when you have a large financial stake in a business, a business plan is invaluable in helping you clarify your goals, organize your finances, and set up long-term goals for growing your business. Plus, a business plan helps you put all your goals, needs, and other considerations down on paper.

> Setting up your business will be more or less complex depending on what kind of enterprise you are planning—grooming dogs in your garage, for example, will be less of an undertaking than opening up your own shop in a separate retail space.

But what about the home groomer who wants to start that part-time operation in the basement through word of mouth? A business plan makes sense for you too, for all the same reasons. You also need to plan. What

will you charge people? How much will equipment cost? Have you thought about how many clients you can handle and how much money you plan to make?

A business plan puts your goals into perspective, from small to large. Include everything from a specific list of what equipment you will need to a ten-year income/expense forecast. Everything you do once you launch your business will go more smoothly if you've thought about it beforehand and written down a plan.

Many resources exist to help you write a business plan. Most towns and cities have at least one small business resource center, often a branch of the government's Small Business Administration (SBA). These centers are definitely worth a visit for the resources and help (often free!) that they provide. No matter how small or informal your grooming business, you will undoubtedly get some sound and helpful information. Besides, who knows how you may decide to expand your business later. Those who think ahead are less likely to encounter unfortunate surprises.

The Internet and the library are other good resources for small business information of all kinds, including business plan writing. You should be able to find lots of sample business plans to give you an idea of format and content. Read over examples of business plans so that you get a feel for what to include. You can also buy software that will help you write a good business plan.

> A business plan is invaluable in helping you clarify your goals, organize your finances, and set up long-term goals for growing your business.

As you educate yourself about becoming self-employed (even if it is only on the side, in addition to your "regular" job), you can expand and tweak your business plan. Type your plan into a computer and print it out. Proofread to be sure that it is correct and professional-looking. Then, if you do

Beauty Tip

The Small Business Administration's (SBA) website contains an outline of a sample business plan and great advice for how to write a plan to submit to a bank if you need a small business loan. Check out this helpful information at www.sba.gov.

decide to take the leap and get a small business loan, you'll be ready.

Your business plan can take any form you want, but it should probably include the following information. Title each section separately, as appropriate for your particular goals:

Summary Statement

This section sets out your overall purpose. In a few pages, describe exactly what your business will be. Who is involved, what will you do, where will you do it, and how many clients do you envision having? Keep this part succinct and informational, summarizing but not going into detail about where you will groom, what services you will offer, how much money you will need to get started, etc.

Growth Plan

In this section, set up a schedule. Begin with where you are right now in terms of getting started. Then, describe your goal for this year, next year, five years, and ten years down the line. Be specific in your goals for clients, space, equipment, and income. Sure, you don't know how things will turn out, but if you have goals, you will have a better chance of shaping your business into exactly what you want within a realistic timeframe.

All About You

In this section, detail your own experience, training, and other qualifications. Did you attend grooming school? Did you apprentice under someone? Are you just getting started in your plan? Write about how you know what you know, or be specific about your plans for furthering your knowledge and experience in the field of grooming. If you will have a business partner or employees, give each person a separate paragraph and discuss that individual's qualifications: knowledge, experience, training, and/or plans for further training.

What You Will Offer

In this section, explain in detail exactly what your business will provide to clients. Will you be a bathing operation only? A full-service groomer for pets? In detail, list the specific services you plan

to provide and how much you plan to charge for them. What will you do and what won't you do? Decide what your hours will be or whether you will groom by appointment only. Will you have a shop front with parking or a separate entrance to your home? How far ahead can people schedule appointments?

Also discuss what equipment and products you will use on pets. Will you make those products for sale, or will you be strictly a service operation and not a retail store? Also decide what extras you will offer. Training? Veterinary referrals? A free grooming session with every ten, or other incentives for regular clients? Remember, you can always add to this section as you learn more.

Your Clients

In this section, discuss who you envision your client base to be. Will you have a high-end boutique-style shop for fancy cuts and show dogs? Or maybe you will cater to the hunting dogs in your rural area or the pampered toy dogs in the neighboring high-rise apartments. Be specific about whom you plan to serve. If you live in a small town, perhaps you will offer all-purpose grooming to the general population. Or if you plan to cater to a niche market, explain that here.

This is also the section to report a little research. How many other groomers work in your area? Are there mobile groomers? In-home groomers? Grooming shops? Where are they located

Your growth plan should specifically outline your goals for clients, space, equipment, and income.

compared to your shop? Also, if possible, compile statistics about how many pets live in your area to determine whether you will fill a need. If you are trying to get a loan from a bank, it will want to know that your shop isn't superfluous and that you will actually be able to attract customers.

The Bottom Line

Finally, it's time to talk money. How much money do you have, how much will you need to get started, and how much do you plan to make? What will you charge for various services? What are your estimated operating expenses? If you plan to borrow money, what will you use it for? Break that down in detail.

If you are planning to get a loan, you can also include your own financial

Brush Up On the Stats

According to a recent survey conducted by PetGroomer.com:

- 56% of home groomers wait at least two years between price increases.
- 60% of home groomers do not discount their services whatsoever.
- 89% of home groomers do not accept credit cards for services rendered.

Be sure to break down your financial bottom line in detail and decide whether you will need to take out a loan.

A grooming shop necessitates some very specific space requirements.

very specific requirements for space. You must have enough room, enough electrical power, a convenient source of water, and sufficient lighting. You should have a customer waiting area, a separate bathing and drying area, and a separate clipping/trimming area.

It's much better to find a space in the beginning that works, that will meet a growing need for electricity and water, that is easy to clean and sanitize (for instance, tiled instead of carpeted), and that has enough room to move around without bumping into walls or other employees. Also, be sure that the space you are considering is properly zoned and that you are aware of all the necessary local codes and other regulations that would apply to a business with heavy electrical and water use and that permits animals. What will happen if dogs soil on the sidewalk or urinate on the building? What will happen if barking bothers neighboring tenants? Look into all the options *before* signing a lease!

If you plan to groom at home, you will probably need to have a dedicated space. Does the basement have enough light? Is the garage warm enough? Is the garden shed large enough? Are you prepared for the cost of increased water and electricity? And can you install a tub, set up a grooming table, put in drying cages, and keep the area sufficiently cool when blow-dryers are running in July?

information here: how much you make, how much you owe, your credit history, etc.

PLAN YOUR SPACE

A business plan is only as good as your own planning about what exactly you will need to set up shop, and that includes looking closely at some of the bare bones of running your own business. A grooming shop in particular necessitates some

MAKE A GROOMING EQUIPMENT WISH LIST

Maybe you dream of a vacuum attachment for your clipper to conveniently suck away unwanted hair, but for now you know that you'll have to make due with regular clippers and a broom. Maybe you wish for a hydraulic tub, but for now, you will have to lift those big dogs as well as you can. Yet you know that you will invest in the best possible

set of professional scissors, a spacious grooming table, and an industrial-strength cage dryer.

You can hire someone to figure out your tax situation, or you can figure it out on your own.

Whatever your priorities, make a detailed list of the equipment you know you will need right away and an additional grooming equipment "wish list" of products you plan to attain eventually. Having these items on paper and planning ahead for when you would like to purchase them will help you when you see a real deal on a hydraulic tub or a vacuum attachment for those clippers. You can follow, or adjust, your financial plan accordingly, knowing that you aren't making purchases on a whim.

PAY YOUR TAXES

As someone who is self-employed, remember that you will also have to pay taxes. No one will be withholding state or federal income tax from your paycheck if you are your own boss. This means that you have to pay taxes yourself. You can hire someone to figure out your tax situation or you can do it on your own, but in most cases, you will need to pay quarterly taxes (pre-paying your

Planning Your Future

It's exciting to think about your future as an independent business owner, a pet groomer setting your own hours and working with animals. Just remember that any successful business takes a lot of work, dedication, self-discipline, and especially careful planning.

amount due in April), which will include a special self-employment tax made just for those of us who work for ourselves. This can add up, so don't forget to include those quarterly tax payments in your budget.

GROW YOUR BUSINESS

Even if you are merely daydreaming about opening a grooming business today, consider that if you do start grooming from home, your grooming business may well grow. Groomers are in high demand! How would you handle a burgeoning business? Would you plan to put a limit on clients, or would you prefer to expand and even hire employees eventually?

If the latter, consider how you might be able to add on to your home or otherwise expand to meet future needs. Could you add on to the garage or put a grooming shop addition onto your house?

ADVERTISE

Speaking of growing your business, how will people know about you? Do you plan to take out an ad in the local paper? Invest in a Yellow Pages listing? Install a sign outside your shop? Design a logo and include it on everything—your sign, your business cards, your stationary, your invoices. Consider, in detail, your plans for marketing your business, small or large. You might be the best groomer for a hundred miles around, but if nobody knows about you, your skills won't do anybody any good.

Think of ways to advertise your grooming services; business cards, for example, are a great way to spread the word.

SAFETY AND LIABILITY ISSUES

Running your own pet grooming business can be profitable, fun, and satisfying. However, like any other business, it has risks that come with the rewards. Many aspects of pet grooming can quickly turn into safety and/or liability issues, but the pet groomer who is prepared for these issues will handle them, should they arise, in the best possible way.

This chapter isn't meant to be a comprehensive discussion of every single thing that could possibly go wrong with your business. Instead, consider it a place to start building your awareness of your responsibility both as a small business owner and the temporary caretaker of animals cherished by others.

This chapter is also not meant to be a source of legal advice. I am not a lawyer and cannot advise you on legal issues. Instead, this chapter is intended to alert you to some of the many safety, liability, and legal issues that could potentially arise for a pet groomer. Should you find yourself in a situation in which you require legal counsel, please seek a qualified professional.

PUT IT IN WRITING

Something about a visual helps everybody understand things better. When you first start grooming, you may be tempted to ask people what they think is a "fair" price, or you may be tempted to give friends a different, lower price. Even when they don't mean to, however, people will take advantage of this kind of "casual" service. If you act like a professional from the beginning, most people won't consider or expect a special deal.

Post your services and the cost of each so that they are clearly visible, either in a brochure or on a sign (or both). If people can look and see exactly how much a bath costs or how much different clips are, they won't argue. When people know exactly

Decide on what you will charge for your grooming services, and distribute your price list to prevent problems.

If you don't want to invest in a fancy price board, something as simple as a chalkboard will work well.

what to expect, they are more likely to be satisfied with the result.

Also, pictures of different clips on the walls make it easy for pet owners to point and say, "I want that." (Be sure that you post only those clips you know how to do!) Describe your services so that people can see what, exactly, they are getting for their money, and don't be afraid to describe special high-end equipment or products you use. List choices of products and prices of each—say, a basic shampoo may be one price, but a special whitening or darkening shampoo may be a slightly higher price. Will you charge more for a hand-scissoring than a quick all-over clip? State that on your price list and describe the difference.

Whose Dog Is This?

Every groomer should have a system to ensure that dogs are returned to their proper owners. Although you may not believe that you could make such a mistake, two dogs of the same breed can look a lot alike. Consider writing up a ticket for each dog as he comes in and keeping that ticket with the dog throughout the entire grooming process. Or maybe have a color-coded system. Whatever your system, just make sure that you have one.

Printing brochures isn't nearly the complicated and expensive job it once was. All you need is a personal computer and a printer. Design a brochure yourself using one of many user-friendly software programs. If you don't want to invest in a fancy price board for your store, consider a dry-erase board or chalkboard, both of which are easy to revise and update.

In other words, let customers read for themselves exactly what you can provide for them and how much it will cost. If anything should happen such that a customer is dissatisfied, you'll be in a more solid position to defend yourself if you can point to the brochure and say "This is what you asked for and this is what I did."

SAFETY FIRST!

You work with water, slippery floors, and electronic equipment. You also work with animals that possess sharp teeth and claws. Put them all together and you have the potential for accidents! Even if you don't hire employees, you should take every precaution to keep yourself from becoming injured. If you get hurt, you can't do your job. (And those small business loan payments aren't going to make themselves.)

Every shop and in-home grooming business is different. Designing a safe workplace depends on the design of your shop, your equipment choices, and to a large extent, how well you keep things cleaned up, maintained, and operating correctly. Keeping your work environment safe requires a little planning and a lot of maintenance. To create and maintain a safe workplace, follow (or adapt as appropriate) the following, adding anything else that is relevant to your unique situation.

For safety reasons, always mop any water off the floor immediately.

Structural Safety

- Be sure that you have enough electrical outlets to handle your electricity load.
- Put filters in drains to catch pet hair to help prevent plumbing problems.
- Carry insurance on your house/shop to cover fire, weather damage, theft, vandalism, etc.

Your Safety

- Always mop any water off the floor immediately—don't wait! If you can't do it, delegate the task right away.
- Apply nonskid surfaces, such as rubber matting that is easy to pull up and hose off if necessary, to floors in heavy-traffic areas.
- Sit whenever possible. You'll be on your feet enough!
- Use tools that feel comfortable. Professional tools tend to be more ergonomic and easier on your hands.
- Keep scissors and blades sharp for ease of use.
- Invest in the quietest possible equipment to preserve your own hearing and for the least possible stress. (Pet grooming gets loud enough!)
- Remember that grooming products, especially those containing pest control chemicals, can cause skin reactions. Wear gloves to protect your skin.
- Wear eye protection.

Brush Up On the Stats

According to a recent survey conducted by PetGroomer.com:

- 62% of groomers do not have a price list to distribute to clients.
- 98% of mobile groomers do not advertise their prices.

Ask the Groomer

Q: Should I hire an accountant to help me manage my business finances?

A: Depending on your motivation, time, and confidence, you may be able to do your own taxes with tax software designed for the small business owner. For some, though, an accountant is well worth the price, to help ensure that your small business return is prepared correctly. But don't depend on your accountant to come up with every possible deduction. That's up to you. Save your receipts and keep careful track of your categorized income and expenses like equipment, products, rent, and utilities. Even if you groom from home, you should be able to deduct a portion of your home expenses as business expenses.

- Attend pet trade shows to keep abreast of the latest in safe and ergonomic equipment and products.

Pet Safety

- Always examine pets before you groom them. If a pet appears sick or injured in any way, don't groom him. Instead, alert the owner. Have a clearly stated policy in your brochure or on a sign that states that you will not groom sick or injured pets. Calling attention to any problems before you groom can help the owner seek veterinary attention for her pet. It will also keep you from getting blamed for a pre-existing condition.
- Avoid electrocution risk—never bathe pets near electrical appliances/tools, and be sure that your

clipping station isn't right next to the bathing station.

- Pay attention to your work while clipping and scissoring. Don't watch television, listen to music, or chitchat, risking pet injury.
- Change clipper blades often so that they don't overheat and burn pets.
- Use nonskid surfaces in tubs and on grooming tables.
- Always secure pets in tubs and on grooming tables with collar/leash assemblies.
- Be prepared for the possibility of dogfights—not all dogs get along, and all pets must be secured to prevent disaster.
- Don't put it past that wet dog to leap out of the tub and out the front door. Always secure uncaged pets. A double door—one leading to a foyer, a second leading to the outside—can also help foil a runaway.

YOUR LIABILITY

But what if, despite your best efforts, something does go wrong? Are you liable? Chances are you could be. Any business that involves clients and their beloved pets, not to mention equipment use, has the potential for liability, and any small business owner should be aware of liability issues. This is why every professional pet groomer should have 1) an attorney, and 2) adequate insurance coverage. From paperwork issues to lawsuits, an attorney can help you handle any legal issues appropriately and with minimum risk to you.

Do you need a business license? Should you be a sole proprietorship or a corporation? Your attorney can help you with these questions. Should you sign that lease? Buy that policy? Do you apologize to the pet owner who unleashed her own dog on your property and her dog was struck by a car? And what about that complaint from your neighbor about barking dogs or that lawsuit your client is threatening because you accidentally nicked her show dog with scissors? Don't answer that—ask your attorney first! Owning your own business is a complicated, well…business! A professional legal advisor isn't a luxury but a necessity.

Whether you've launched a burgeoning local retail establishment or are perfectly content to groom the pets of a few friends in your basement, make safety a priority to help prevent liability issues. If that means grooming a little bit slower or spending a little more on equipment, cleanup, electrical work, or plumbing, remember that your extra time and care will only enhance your reputation as a safe, responsible, caring professional.

Remember that you went into this business because you love dogs and want to work with them and help them be healthier and more beautiful. That's great! But that also means paying attention, being careful, using the best possible equipment, not taking on more than you can handle, taking responsibility for your actions and your work, and finally, protecting both your clients and yourself with clear policies, good insurance coverage, legal backup, and your very best work. What more could a pet owner want from a groomer?

And as your clients become more loyal, as your client base grows, and as your shop expands, you'll wonder how you could have ever tolerated any other job. You are a pet groomer, and you are great at your job because you never stop learning, growing, and improving.

Congratulations on achieving your career goal!

GLOSSARY

angulation: The angles formed by the different joints in the skeleton

apple head: A rounded, domed skull, such as that in the Chihuahua

bat ear: An erect, broad-at-the-base ear, such as in the French Bulldog

beard: The thick, long hair on the underjaw, such as on a Schnauzer

bitch: A female canine

bite: The position of the upper and lower teeth when the jaws are closed

blaze: A white stripe running down the center of the face, often between the eyes

bloom: The sheen of a healthy coat

blue: A coat color resulting in a genetically diluted black coat

bracelets: The rounded tufts of hair on the back legs of the Poodle in a Continental clip or English Saddle clip

brachycephalic: The condition of having a flat face, short nose, and elongated soft palate, sometimes resulting in respiratory problems and always resulting in a low heat tolerance

breed standard: The official written description of how a particular breed should look

brindle: A coat pattern characterized by layered black with a lighter color, resembling a tiger stripe

brokenhaired: A harsh, wiry coat; also called wirehaired

brows: The bony ridges above the eyes, left covered in tufted hair in some breeds

brush tail: A bushy or heavily coated tail

bur: The inside of the ear

button ear: An ear that folds forward with the tip lying close to the skull to cover the ear opening

canines: The two upper and two lower larger, pointed teeth between the incisors and the premolars

cape: The thick, more heavily coated area of coat over the shoulders, occurring in many breeds

carpals: Wrist bones

cat foot: A round, compact food with arched, tight toes

clip: The particular cut or trim of the coat in breeds whose coat allows for different styles, such as a Poodle, Bichon Frise, or Schnauzer

clipped/shaved bands: The shaved areas between bracelets (q.v.) on the back legs of a Poodle

coat: The hair that covers a dog's skin, either single, or in many

breeds, a double coat with an outer and undercoat

condition: How a dog looks overall, including coat, skin, muscle tone, and behavior

conformation: The physical attributes of the dog; the shape, structure, outline, etc., as described in the official written breed standard for that breed

crescents: Curved, clipped areas on the flanks of a Poodle in the English Saddle clip

cropping: The cutting of the ear leather to make the ears stand up or have a particular appearance

culotte: The long hair on the backs of the legs of some breeds

dapple: A mottled coat pattern of dark patterns over light, characteristic of some breeds such as Dachshunds

dentition: The way in which the teeth are arranged; also the quality and number of teeth. (Adult dogs should have 42 teeth.)

dewclaw: The vestigial "toe" on the inside of the leg. Pet owners and breeders sometimes have the dewclaws surgically removed by a veterinarian.

dewlap: The loose, hanging skin on the throat of some breeds

docking: The cutting of a tail after birth to shorten it

dog: A term used by breeders to refer to male dogs

double coat: A common type of coat in many breeds, in which the outercoat is harsher and weather resistant, while the undercoat is softer and downier for warmth

drop ears: Ears that drop down to the sides or are otherwise folded over

erect ears: Ears that stand straight up or point out at an angle. Also called "prick ears."

fall: Hair that hangs over the face, an appropriate style in some breeds.

feathering: Wispy feathers of hair in a coat.

flag tail: A long fringed tail carried high like a flag

fluffies: A long, overly feathered coat, considered a fault in the show ring

fringes: Feathering

furnishings: Long hair on the extremities (head, tail, and legs) of some breeds

gazehound: Another word for "sighthound"

hackles: The part of the coat on the back and neck that raises when the dog is afraid or on the alert

hare foot: A type of foot in which the two middle "toes" are noticeably longer than the outer and inner toe; this kind of foot appears relatively long, like a rabbit's foot.

harlequin: A coat pattern of black or gray patches over white

herding dogs: Any of the breeds that herds cattle, sheep, or even waterfowl; as pets, these breeds may herd cats, children, or other dogs. Examples include Border Collies, German Shepherd Dogs, Old English Sheepdogs, and Pulis.

hound: A dog used to hunt by sight or scent

hound-marked: The bi-colored or tri-colored coat pattern common to many hound breeds (and some other breeds), characterized by a white background with tan and/or black marks on the head, back, legs, and tail. The exact location of marks varies by breed and individual.

isabella: A fawn color characteristic of some breeds such as Dachshunds and Doberman Pinschers

leather: The ear flap

liver: A deep reddish brown coat color

mane: The long thick hair over the neck, characteristic of some breeds such as Chow Chows and Pomeranians.

marcel coat: Continuous waves, as in some American Water Spaniels

merle: A mottled coat pattern of dark streaks over light that is characteristic of some breeds such as Collies

mottled: A coat pattern of dark round marks on a lighter background, as with the Australian Cattle Dog

non-sporting dogs: An American Kennel Club (AKC) group of breeds that don't fit into other categories such as Sporting, Toy, or Working. Examples include the Bichon Frise, Chinese Shar-Pei, Chow Chow, Dalmatian, and Lhasa Apso.

particolored: A coat pattern of two or more mottled colors occurring in patches; also called pied or piebald.

pastern: The front leg between the wrist and toes.

pedigree: The written record of a dog's ancestry, tracing back relatives for at least three generations

peppering: White and black hairs mixed together

pied: Large patches of at least two colors; also called piebald or parti-colored.

prick ears: Ears that stand straight up or point out at an angle; also called "erect ears."

roan: Colored and white hairs finely intermingled

ruff: The longer, thick haircoat around the neck, shoulders, and chest of some breeds; also called the mane.

sable: A coat of black-tipped hairs on a background of silver, gray, fawn, or brown

saddle: A black, saddle-shaped mark over the back

scenthound: Any of the breeds that hunts by smell, including Basset Hounds, Beagles, and Bloodhounds

semi-prick ears: Erect ears with only the tips falling forward

sighthound: Any of the breeds that hunts by sight, including Afghan Hounds, Greyhounds, and Whippets

smooth coat: A short, close coat

splayfoot: A flat foot with spread-out toes. Failure to keep the nails short can cause a splayfoot and compromise foot health.

sporting dogs: Any of the breeds designed to flush, point, and/or retrieve birds for hunters; also called gundogs. Examples include Cocker Spaniels, German Shorthaired Pointers, Irish Setters, and Labrador Retrievers.

standoff coat: A long, heavy coat that stands out from the body

stifle: The rear leg "knee" joint

stop: The angle between the skull and muzzle, more pronounced in some dogs than others

terriers: Any of the small to medium-sized breeds, mostly developed in the British Isles, designed to catch vermin

ticked: Small, isolated colored patches on a white background

topknot: A long tuft of hair on the top of the head

topline: The dorsal surface of the dog. In some breeds, the topline is level, and in others, it slopes up or down.

toy dogs: Any of the breeds designed to serve as small companions to humans, such as Maltese, Pekingese, Shih Tzu, Toy Poodles, and Yorkshire Terriers.

wheaten: A pale yellow color

whitelies: A white body with red or dark markings, as in the Pembroke Welsh Corgi.

wirehair: A hard, crisp, wiry coat

wirehaired: A rough, wiry coat; also called brokenhaired or broken-coated.

working dogs: Any of the breeds designed to guard, pull heavy carts or sleds, or do other heavy-duty work, including Doberman Pinschers, Great Danes, Rottweilers, and Siberian Huskies

RESOURCES

ASSOCIATIONS AND ORGANIZATIONS

American Kennel Club (AKC)
5580 Centerview Drive
Raleigh, NC 27606
Telephone: (919) 233-9767
Fax: (919) 233-3627
E-Mail: info@akc.org
www.akc.org

Canadian Kennel Club (CKC)
89 Skyway Avenue, Suite 100
Etobicoke, Ontario M9W 6R4
Telephone: (416) 675-5511
Fax: (416) 675-6506
E-Mail: information@ckc.ca
www.ckc.ca

International Professional
Groomers, Inc. (IPG)
www.ipgicmg.com

Federation Cynologique
Internationale (FCI)
Secretariat General de la FCI
Place Albert 1er, 13
B – 6530 Thuin
Belqique
www.fci.be

National Dog Groomers
Association of America, Inc.
(NDGAA)
www.nationaldoggroomers.com

The International Society of
Canine Cosmetologists (ISCC)
2702 Covington Drive
Garland, TX 75040

www.petstylist.com

The Kennel Club
1 Clarges Street
London
W1J 8AB
Telephone: 0870 606 6750
Fax: 0207 518 1058
www.the-kennel-club.org.uk

United Kennel Club (UKC)
100 E. Kilgore Road
Kalamazoo, MI 49002-5584
Telephone: (269) 343-9020
Fax: (269) 343-7037
E-Mail: pbickell@ukcdogs.com
www.ukcdogs.com

BOOKS

De Vito, Dominique, et al. *World Atlas of Dog Breeds.* 6th Ed. Neptune City: TFH Publications, Inc., 2009.

TFH Publications, Inc. *All 87 Breed Dog Grooming.* Revised Ed. Neptune City: TFH Publications, Inc., 1995.

TFH Publications, Inc. *All-Breed Dog Grooming.* Revised Ed. Neptune City: TFH Publications, Inc., 1987, 2010.

Whitehead, Sarah. *Pamper Your Pooch.* Neptune City: TFH Publications, Inc., 2007.

Young, Peter. *Groom Your Dog Like a Professional.* Neptune City: TFH Publications, Inc., 2009.

PERIODICALS

Dog Fancy
www.dogfancy.com

Groomer to Groomer
www.groomertogroomer.com

WEBSITES

www.findagroomer.com
This easy-to-use resource helps you locate professional groomers in your area.

www.fourpaws.com
A great source for grooming supplies and more for your pet.

www.nylabone.com
Chews, toys, treats, and more to keep your dog occupied and happy while you groom him.

www.petgroomer.com
This website has everything from lists of grooming schools to specific directions on grooming different breeds to advice on setting up your own business. An excellent resource for groomers of any level.

www.tfh.com
Find some of the best books on grooming available today.

INDEX

Boldfaced numbers
indicate illustrations.